LIl
THE LANC/

by
Janet Rigby

Landy Publishing

2006

ISBN 1 872895 66 2

A catalogue record of this book is available from the British
Library.

Layout by Janet Rigby
Printed by Nayler Group Ltd. Accrington.
Tel: 01254 234247

Landy Publishing have also published:

Northward by Anthony Hewitson
Glimpses of Glasson Dock by Ruth Z Roskell
Preston in Focus by Stephen Sartin
Penwortham, Longton & Hutton by Catherine Rees
Traipsing from a Lancashire Toll Bar by Betty Gilkes & Stan
Pickles
Lancashire's Medieval Monasteries by Brian Marshall
Play Up, Higher Walton by Peter Holme
Cockersand Abbey by Brian Marshall

A full list is available from:

Landy Publishing
'Acorns' 3 Staining Rise, Staining, Blackpool, FY3 0BU
Tel/Fax: 01253 895678

INTRODUCTION

My interest in writing this book arose through my family's link with the Lancaster Canal, often called the 'Preston to Kendal Canal'.

My husband David's great grandfather Charles, 1858 – 1910 was from the Ashcroft family who were connected with the canal from almost the beginning. His son George was the last boatman of this particular branch which ended with his death on the Somme in 1916. Charles's brother Joseph (1853 – 1912) was the grandfather of Dan, Joe and Jack Ashcroft who were the last of the Ashcrofts to sail the 'Lanky' (the nickname for the Lancaster Canal). Charles's granddaughter Mildred Rigby (nee Lomax) aged 92 still remembers the Sunday school outings on the converted canal boats in the 1920's and lives in a house backing on to the canal at Preston, near the terminus at Ashton basin.

However, this is not a one-family history; it is intended to look into the lives of the many people who were the backbone of the waterway until commercial trade ceased in 1947, the people who lived and worked on them, the boats themselves, and the sad fate of many that were broken up and lost for ever.

I am indebted to many people who have assisted me in my research, amongst them Cyril Thompson, Dorothy Green, Colin Barnes, Pam Paget-Tomlinson, Mike Clarke, Mike Taylor, Tony Lewery, Trevor Hughes, John Gavan and David Slater of the Lancaster Canal Trust, and many others. A special mention goes to Mary Moulding for the loan of the tapes of her late father John Tickle. I am also indebted to John Parkinson, one of the 'younger boatmen' on the Lancaster Canal whose recorded tapes provided me with a wealth of information. His knowledge of canals is remarkable, he is definitely the 'oracle' on not only the Lancaster but all the North West canals.

Janet Rigby – February 2006

A plan of the Lancaster Canal submitted to the Committee by William Cartwright in 1799

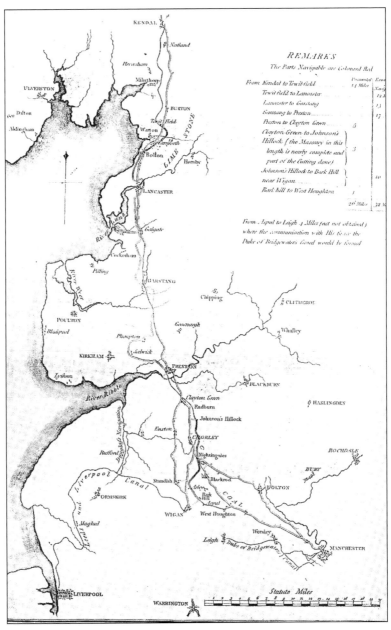

THE CANAL IN PRESTON IN THE EARLY DAYS

It is said that Charles Dickens, who visited Preston in February 1854, based his fictitious grimy *'Coketown' in 'Hard Times'* on Preston, the very model of a Lancashire cotton mill town. *"It was a town of red brick, or of brick that would have been red if the smoke and ashes had allowed it…it was a town of machinery and tall chimneys, out of which interminable serpents of smoke trailed themselves for ever and ever, and never got uncoiled. It had a black canal in it, and a river that ran purple with ill-smelling dye…."* The *"black canal"* referred to in the passage could only be the Preston – Kendal canal.

In 1843 a reformer, the Reverend John Clay had reported the poor state of the town's dwellings and mentioned the following areas in particular: which were near the canal basin. *"There is in the lowest deep a lower deep and in the districts of the worst kind there are certain streets and courts etc. of the worst of the district. The names of these are Canal Street, Back Canal Street, Hope Street, Holden's Square, Holdens Yard, Edward Street, Buckingham Street, Clarence Street, Poplar Street, Willow Street, Queen Street and Savages Court."*

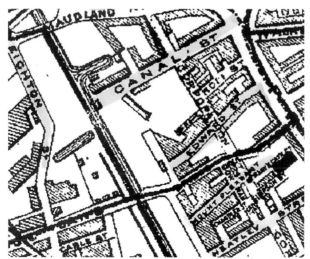

Canal wharf and surrounding streets from Brown's Map of Preston 1889

Some of these dwellings were inhabited by canal boatmen's families and were often left empty for periods when the family were working on the canal. In 1861 the census enumerator drew particular attention to the Hope Street area, in the St Peter's Chapelry and described it as *"one of the poorest and most neglected district in Preston.......... The cottages are very dirty and miserable. Indeed there is such an entire absence of social comfort, that few respectable persons would imagine there was such an amount of misery and destitution in Preston".*

When Daniel Ashcroft, one of the earlier boatmen and Elizabeth Beesley married in 1847, their homes were in Hope Street and Back Edward Street. These streets were classed as a *"very unfavourable place to live"* and were formerly cellared handloom weavers' cottages, mostly cleared in 1884 – 1900. The area is now occupied by the University of Central Lancashire.

In 1850, the sanitation of the town was in a very poor state. There was the eternal problem of getting rid of human waste from the *'privies'* in these back to back houses, which if not disposed of properly, spread disease among the inhabitants and was probably one of the main causes of the cholera epidemic which hit Preston in 1849. At the first outbreak of cholera in the country in 1848, a Sanitation Committee was set up in Preston on 23 October, appointing a police sergeant as *'Inspector of Nuisances'* at a wage of twenty three shillings a week.

Under cover of darkness

Daniel Vickers, whose family were boatmen on the Lancaster and Leeds – Liverpool canals, offered to get out eighty tons of night soil per night and take it away by canal each evening, free of charge, an offer which was eagerly accepted. It was not long before Daniel was the subject of a *'case of nuisance'* and was brought before the Sanitary Committee, accused of causing unnecessary spillage from his cart in the area of Winckley Square. This area housed the professional and property owning classes, who not surprisingly complained of an intolerable stench.   The job of night soil man was a nasty job for anyone and such was the nature of the job that had to be done by darkness so that the people responsible albeit with inefficient and leaky carts and lack of light could carry out the work in a hygienic way.

These carts, sometimes referred to as *'treacle wagons'* were totally unfit for the job and Mr Vickers was asked why he did not go down Avenham Street. He replied, *"I did, sir"*. Mr Gorst, the Court clerk said, *"Then you divided your favours"*. Mr Vickers was then ordered to pay costs and donate *"half a crown to the poor box."*

The terminus at Preston

Preston Terminus of the Lancaster Canal.
Taken from an etching in Hewitson's *History of Preston* – 1883.

The canal basin was constructed around 1804 and was formed at a point forty yards from the end of the main canal, extending for 100 yards in an easterly direction. The north side was designated a public wharf and the south side set out for the limestone trade, the coal yards being situated closer to Fishergate. Buildings used as warehouses dated back to 1798 and were mostly demolished in 1938. The actual terminus basin now lies buried under a superstore complex in Corporation Street, along with the broken up remains of many working boats, showing few traces of its former presence.

The starting place for the boats was the basin at Leighton Street. Before loading at the coal tip the boats were manoeuvred into an area known as *"the muck fields,"* so called because of the refuse from the neighbourhood tipped there to be loaded into the boats and taken to farmers along the canal for manure.

From the wharf there were two small branches, one leading towards Leighton Street, and the other towards Corporation Street in the opposite direction which had a yard where boats were pulled onto a

7

slipway for repair. The streets leading down to the canal where some of the boatmen's families lived (Back Canal Street, Mount Pleasant, Nixons Row, Edward Street and others) have mostly now gone.

The southern end of the Preston Basin 1938

The terminus at Preston is now *'Ashton basin'* situated approximately one mile north from the original one. This section is often referred to as the *'lost mile'* though some traces of the canal can still be seen. The *'Lime Kiln'* public house stands near to the site of the lime kiln in Aqueduct Street where the limestone rock would be transhipped to the kiln where it was burned to a fine powder before being either spread across the fields or combined with sand to form mortar for building works.

The line of the canal from Fylde Road bridge, near the *'Watering Trough'* public house is now grassed over. This leads up to the university which is situated near to the original canal basin. Along Marsh Lane is the *'Boatman's Arms,'* a public house that once provided stabling for the horses in its outbuildings. There is an archway leading to the rear with lettering still evident *'Good Stabling Here'*.

Mary Ashcroft in stables at Boatman's Arms

J H Spencer, the Preston historian, wrote in the Preston Herald in 1944:- *"The best navigable stretch of the canal is from Maudland Bridge to the terminus near the top of Marsh Lane and from here it is wider and the water deeper and cleaner than elsewhere. This has been made so as to allow for the passage and anchorage of barges at the long wharves at either side where the loading and unloading takes place."*

In 1954, several years after the closure of the canal to commercial traffic, it was recorded in the *'Lancashire Evening Post'* that part of the canal could soon be closed to navigation and the public by an Act of Parliament probably between half and three quarters of a mile from the Marsh Lane end. Demolition of the aqueduct bridge was included in the scheme.

A Dastardly Outrage

A dramatic incident had occurred way back in 1887, which could have had drastic consequences on the town if an attempt to blow up the aqueduct bridge stone archway by *'anarchists'* had not been foiled. Millions of gallons of water would have flooded Preston as its inhabitants slept. Thomas Hesketh, a labourer, arrived for work as usual that morning at the lime kilns which were at the time situated opposite the Lime Kiln Inn in Aqueduct Street. He noticed a small iron pipe with what appeared to be a piece of string attached leaning against a hoarding by the bridge. His boss, who realised what it was, discovered a rubber cartridge attached to a long length of fuse. The police were immediately called and they confirmed that there was enough dynamite to blow up at least thirty tons of stone masonry and earth but it was clearly the work of an amateur and would not have been successful.

The *'Lancashire Daily Post'* headlines read *'Dastardly Outrage in Preston'* and went on to say *"The aqueduct is one of the latest in the country and has been strengthened from time to time, but is not of great stability. The canal overhead stretches from Preston to Kendal and before the flow of water escaping from it could have been stopped damage would have been incalculable and the loss of life very great."*

At the time of the explosion attempt, two groups under suspicion were the *'Preston Republican Society'* and the *'Fenians'* a secret Irish organisation dedicated to overthrowing British rule, who were active in Preston at that time but neither organisation was ever positively linked to the canal aqueduct sabotage attempt. In 1964 the aqueduct was demolished when the first three quarters of a mile at the Preston end was finally drained and infilled.

Drainage

Part of the canal was drained in 1959 and it appeared that it had been a convenient tip for disposal of unwanted items such as prams, tyres and household furniture. My husband recalls when he was a small boy in the 1950's, he and his brother, armed with a butcher's hook, were fishing in the canal close to where he lived to see what they could dredge up. They suddenly had a *'catch'* - a bicycle that looked just like the one their father had recently lost. Excitedly they pulled the bicycle to the canal bank and rushed home with their find. Their father was not pleased, as it had been intended to sink without trace beneath the waters, having been thrown from Roebuck Street bridge quite intentionally.

A massive rescue operation was mounted to save the fish, as a joint effort by the *'North West Water Authority'* and members of the Preston group branch of the *'North West Anglers Association.'* It took several days to pump the millions of gallons of water out of the stretch of canal, which had been dammed under Fylde Road bridge. As the waters started dropping, the volunteer rescuers waded through the thick black mud with nets scooping the wriggling fish into large bowls, carrying them along the bank before releasing them in the higher reaches of the canal.

The canal wharf in 1897

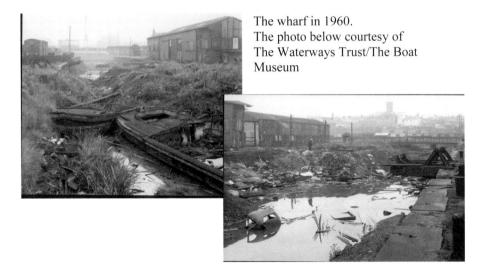

The wharf in 1960.
The photo below courtesy of
The Waterways Trust/The Boat
Museum

11

EARLY CARRIERS FROM PRESTON WHARF

An article by Harry Hansen came to me by courtesy of John Gavan who had been given this account of early days of canal carrying in Preston some years ago. A young boy called Myles Pennington, just about to start his first real job as an apprentice in John Hargreaves' fly boat office in Wharf Street, Preston. These *'high speed'* fly boats carried goods but no passengers between Kendal and Preston, thence by rail over the River Ribble to join the Leeds and Liverpool Canal at Walton Summit.

He wrote, *"Horse drawn carts and wagons laden with goods for delivery in town or at the canal warehouses ground over the cobblestones. From the 'Boatman's Arms' came raucous sounds as watermen recharged before the next trip. More discreet murmurings emerged from the 'Lamb and Packet' where passengers awaited the Lancaster packet boat."*

Myles who was born in Lancaster in 1814, was *'well trained in the art and mystery of canal transport at the Lancaster wharf'* where his father held the job of John Hargreaves' agent. One of his first jobs was to charge out some goods from Manchester – an easy enough task – but he soon found that Preston affairs were not ordered in the same way as in Lancaster.

"Where are the rates?" he asked the agent.
"Oh call in Joe, he knows more about rates."

Joe Hornby, the carter who collected and delivered goods in Preston, *"a clean-shaven rather pleasant looking fellow"* came into the office and *'charging out'* began. *"Joe strokes his hair in front and looks wondrous wise".*

"Tommy Careful, one bale?" queries young Pennington.

"Fourteen pence," says Joe.

"Billy Sharp one bale"

"He'll only stand one shilling".

"Peter Careless, one truss"

"He'll stand eighteen pence"

And so it went on, people paying different rates for the same goods from the same place, according to what a man, in Joe's estimation, would stand. The rates were also based on caste – esquires, reverends, military officers and nobility having to pay for their titles.

"This kind of charging was rather difficult to keep track of," Myles was to write later *"and I made a private rate book, which I kept securely in my drawer."*

A perk of the job
Other aspects of canal management were equally loose at Preston. Alcohol oiled the wheels a great deal and sometimes gummed them up. The story went that one night, all the men at Hargreaves' warehouse, including the agent, got so drunk that no one was in a fit state to take the train of wagons loaded with butter for the Manchester market along the tramway to Walton Summit basin.
Young Myles was faced with a problem and he hurriedly harnessed a team of horses and started out bravely into the night, but his inexperience caused the train to leave the tracks. He roused a farmer and between them they managed to set the precious cargo back on the rails.

"I reached Summit in safety" he related proudly, *"and was received with three cheers by the boatmen."*

One reason for the prevalence of drunkenness in canal offices was that the agent, in the course of his duties, had to take samples from casks of spirits to ensure non-interference in transit. Boatmen were known to have the knack of taking out a gallon of rum from a hogshead and replacing it with water. Strictly speaking these samples belonged to the carrier; in practice they started many on the road to drunkenness.

Hey up!

Wharf men were not usually privy to these *'samples'* but the Preston porters did have one windfall. Packs of wool came down from Scotland and were transhipped at Preston. There were always a few lost their identifying tags. One year some bags were left unclaimed at the end of the season and were being placed in a storeroom. One porter chanced to lie down on a bag – only to jump up abruptly. *"There's a dead man in that bag!"* he cried. They rushed to open it. Not a body, but a ten-gallon keg of Scotch whisky was laid bare. It was being smuggled into England without paying revenue. The porters *'confiscated'* the liquor and, according to Pennington, *"were not fairly sober for a month afterwards"*.

Myles never forgot his employer – John Hargreaves – who would pass by the office every three months. He was a bulky, imposing individual with a broad, heavily-whiskered red face, rather after the stamp of John Bull. He was a man of immense activity, checking regularly on all his stations between Manchester and Edinburgh. He went by stage-coach and would invariably *'take over the tapes.'* (reins). No one was his equal in driving a four horse coach. Hargreaves, a great lover of horses, *"owned more than any other man, and understood more about them"*. Sick animals were sent to his large farm and residence at Hart Common, near Wigan, where he doctored them himself. He was not a man to be trifled with. A tollgate man once quarrelled with him. *"What are you, sir?"* the toll collector demanded disparagingly. *"You are only a common carrier."* *"I am an uncommon carrier,"* thundered back Hargreaves. *"I carry further than any man in England."* But perhaps he met his match in young Myles. Hargreaves was supposed to pay the lad's board bill, clothing etc. and a monthly statement of expenditure furnished by his apprentice. The boy did not care for the system and one day when the carrier boomed in with his traditional *"Well Myles,"* he openly rebelled against it. Hargreaves agreed to pay him sixteen shillings a week – no mean sum when farm labourers were lucky to earn fourteen shillings.

He later became the first goods manager of the *'Preston and Wyre Railway'* and eventually the first general traffic agent of the *'Canadian Grand Trunk Railway'* where he was still at work in 1896 at the age of eighty-two. He was also one of the founder members of the Temperance Movement which started in Preston and was one of its ardent supporters when he was living in Toronto. The story recounted here appeared in his memoirs in a Toronto newspaper.

Early Passenger Carriers

Although the Lancaster canal was primarily intended to carry cargo, in 1798, a passenger service was created as an alternative to the hazardous turnpike roads that existed at the time when the Canal Company advertised:-

Painting of Kendal canal wharf (source unknown)

a *"pleasant voyage from Lancaster to Preston for the Guild"* and declared to the public that *"For safety, economy and comfort, no other mode of conveyance could be so eligible as the packet boats, for there the timid might be at ease and the most delicate mind without fear."* It had been said by business travellers, when asked why they preferred to travel this way, *"Why of course we travel by water, it's fast, much more comfortable than a horse or coach and there are no highwaymen here. There's usually a refreshment counter for food and drinks and with two or three classes we don't have to mix with the poor"*.

They were named *'packet boats'*; a term borrowed from the seafaring world and ran a regular service between Kendal, and Lancaster and Preston from 1st May 1820. The boat left Kendal at 6 am and arrived at Preston, a journey of 57 miles at 8 pm, a fourteen hour journey at 4 miles per hour.

'Waterwitch' (Ruth Roskell collection)

'Swift boats' were the fastest passenger craft, travelling up to fourteen miles per hour behind two galloping horses and were introduced to try and stave off competition from the railways which were being introduced in the early and mid 19th century.

The *'Lamb and Packet'* Hotel situated at the bottom of Friargate still stands today at the north end, in Kendal Street at the head of the former Canal Street and because of its proximity to the canal basin is believed to have been the departure point and ticket office for the packet boats, hence its name. The present inn sign, which is not the original, depicts a lamb gazing at an ocean going *'clipper type'* packet ship. The lamb of course is the symbol of Preston. A handbill advertising the packet boat service in 1833 states that *'places secured from Preston, Legs of Man coach offices, opposite the Town Hall"* and does not mention the Lamb and Packet at all. The *'Legs of Man'* was a public house in Fishergate. Tea, coffee and refreshments were provided along the way and the boats were heated.

The pace of life increases yet further

In 1833 a faster boat *'Waterwitch'* was introduced, running between Kendal and Preston, the whole journey being reduced by half from 14 hours to 7 making a return journey within the day. It went at ten miles per hour, changing the horses every four miles, the changeover taking only seconds to complete. The fare for the single journey was six shillings first class and four shillings second class. A total of 16,000 passengers used the service during six months in 1833. These high speeds were made possible by the small number of locks along the route and the towpath running on one side of the canal almost all the way, only changing once at Lancaster.

Between 1833 and 1835 an observant *"gentleman of leisure"* Sir John Head, took himself on a *"Home Tour of the Manufacturing Districts of England"* and recites the episodes that happened to him with both humour and humanity. On the way back after crossing England he went on the Waterwitch *"a sheet iron boat, a little more than seventy feet long by five feet four inches broad and draws, when light, only six inches of water. The Swiftsure is two feet shorter, four inches narrower, and heavier by about a ton and a half. Notwithstanding the difference in figure, both boats have light canoe-like appearance, and are fitted up in a similar manner, a light awning of stout calico, dressed with linseed oil, effectually protects the passengers from the weather, though it sheds a yellow watery light on the people's countenance. The embarkation at Preston is most commodious. A covered shed, thrown over the canal encloses on both sides ample marginal space, so that passengers and their luggage are equally protected from the rabble and the weather."*

The boats adhered to a strict schedule, so much so that it was said that on one occasion it would not interrupt its journey to search for a missing person who was feared drowned. A body was later found in the water.

The packet boats, likewise flyboats, had right of way over any other craft, having priority at locks and bridges. It was rumoured that the Bridgewater Canal packet boats carried a curved shining blade in the bows to slice through the tow rope of any lesser craft impudent enough to get in the way.

There was a regular fly boat service from Preston up to about 1845 which sailed on regular timings every day. It would start about two in the morning in Preston, would discharge what it had picked up coming down the canal, re-load during the afternoon, accepting

17

cargo up to a certain time and would deliver to warehouses along the canal ready to be distributed. There was a warehouse at Penny Street bridge which was used as a transhipment point for passengers and goods

The design of the *'Waterwitch'* was based on William Houston's swift boats on the Scottish canals. Long and thin, 76 feet by 6 feet maximum beam, canal companies were quick to introduce this innovatory design to English routes. The journey time between Preston and Kendal was cut to ten hours. The *'Waterwitch'* was a resounding success, especially amongst the business and professional classes, having a capacity for up to 120 passengers. Orders for another three boats followed in the next five years. They were pulled by two horses, changed every four or five miles at stable points along the route, the second horse being ridden by a *'postillion'* usually a boy, driving the first horse who would sound his horn to warn of their approach. He would have to stoop quite low on the horse's neck to pass under the low arches of the bridges.

Not fast enough

LANCASTER CANAL.

THE swift sailing PACKET BOATS between LAN-CASTER and KENDAL, SAIL daily as follows:—

From Lancaster ... 7 30 a.m. 12 0
From Kendal ... ... 8 30 do. 1 30 p.m.

The Boats from Lancaster will be despatched on arrival of the respective Trains from the South, and the Boats from Kendal will be in time for the Trains to the South at 1 10 p.m., and 5 30 p.m.

Fares between Lancaster and Kendal, First Cabin, 3s.; Second Cabin, 2s.

Breakfast and Refreshments provided on Board. The Boats are warmed in cold weather.

An Omnibus between the Railway and Packet Stations at Lancaster, free of charge. Aug. 24, 1842.

In 1842 the route between Lancaster and Preston was abandoned, largely due to competition from the railways. From September 1st that year the sailing times between Lancaster and Kendal were changed and a free omnibus provided.

Advertisement. in *'Preston Pilot'* 3 September 1842

The *'Waterwitch'* was taken out of service and was said along with *'Swiftsure'* to have ended its days on the Crinan canal in Scotland but this has not been proved. However, the *'Crewdson'* (named after the Chairman of the Canal Company) and the *'Swiftsure'* ran for another few years until the opening of the Lancaster - Carlisle

18

railway. The *'Crewdson'* was put into storage in the packet boathouse at Aldcliffe Road, Lancaster, and later converted into an inspection boat, its cabin cut down by one third. It was re-named *'Waterwitch II.'* Sadly, this historic boat was later destroyed, although a replica can be seen at Lancaster Maritime Museum.

Packet Boathouse at Aldcliffe

Ruins of Packet Boathouse at Aldcliffe

Kendal terminus

Like Preston the terminus of the *'northern'* end of the canal has now almost completely disappeared. The canal basin was opened on 18 June 1819 and consisted of four wharves on each on its north and south sides, two wharves at its east end and a pair of covered warehouses along its west end. In 1824 the canal company sold some land for Kendal gas works, thus creating a coal traffic which continued for 120 years.

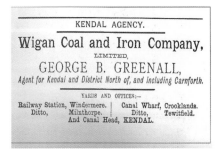

KENDAL AGENCY.

Wigan Coal and Iron Company,

LIMITED,

GEORGE B. GREENALL,

Agent for Kendal and District North of, and including Carnforth.

YARDS AND OFFICES:—

Railway Station, Windermere.	Canal Wharf, Crooklands.
Ditto, Milnthorpe.	Ditto, Tewitfield.
And Canal Head, KENDAL.	

In 1912 three of the four wharves on Canal Head north were still occupied by coal merchants, the Wigan Coal & Iron Company, Samuel Thompson & Co. who also operated from the railway station and Anthony Thompson, both with stables. Wigan Coal & Iron Co. had a stable and stone yard on Canal Head south.

Kendal ticket office (Trevor Hughes)

Coal office c 1900 (Trevor Hughes)

The coal office which stood at the end of Canal Head North on the east side of the beginning of the towpath, now demolished, has a sign which reads *'W. Vickers' Brick & Coal Yard, dealer in Hay and Straw'* c 1900. A similar entry for William Vickers appears in the Bulmer's Trade Directory.

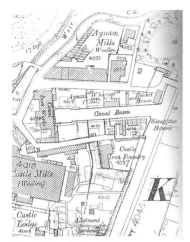

Canal Head, Kendal
District Valuer's Map 1912

Canal Head, Kendal c 1897

On the canal, Kendal

Canal from Parkside Bridge, Kendal

FAMILIES ON THE CANAL

The families that worked the boats on the Lancaster canal were found from the census returns to have mostly been born in Preston, with just a few originating from Lancaster and Kendal. The nature of their working lives brought many of them together, resulting in marriage between families and many were inter-related.

An article appeared in the *'Lancashire Daily Post'* in 1934 written by *'AHG'* the renowned journalist, Arthur Harry Griffin, who visited the wharf behind Corporation Street shortly before *a* convoy of canal boats left Preston for *"a trip to the north and back to have a look over the boats and a chat with the jolly canal folk"* He found that the generations of the families on the canal in the mid thirties *"have followed on for years"* and *"the history of the canal is almost the history of the Baines', the Ashcrofts and the Robinsons; the Baines' of Ladywell Street owning all the canal boats."* and went on to report that *"the oldest member of the Preston contingent at the time was fifty five year old Daniel Ashcroft who has lived and worked all his life on the waterways and has two sons as canal boat 'skippers'."* This was Dan Ashcroft senior and his sons Dan

Dan Ashcroft senior and his wife Alice Goodier

and Joe who with their brother John were the last working boatmen on the Lancaster canal. Dan was born on *'Prince of Wales'* in 1908 at

Crooklands and married Mary Robinson, daughter of Thomas Robinson, bringing together two of the main families on the canal.

In fact AHG wrote admirably of Mrs Elizabeth Ann Robinson, Thomas Robinson's mother saying that she was *'the skipper' of the boat in which she lives with her family and is the only woman navigator on the canal and whose daughter May who was born on the canal and christened after the name of the boat"*. He describes her as *"strong, weather-beaten and buxom and well equipped to do the rough work of the boats."* Elizabeth was the grandmother of John Parkinson and he says that in 1934 she still had three sons and one daughter with her, having been left a widow in 1928 with nine children. The canal boat register also shows a Mrs Robinson, widow, daughters and son on *'Ann'*.

The Ashcroft *'dynasty'* stretched back five generations to the beginning of the 1800s when Dan Ashcroft's great great grandparents Thomas and Jane were on the canal until their deaths in the eighteen fifties. One of their sons, Charles, also a canal boatman, was the father of Daniel and Joseph christened in 1828 at St John's Parish Church, Preston. Their children form two main branches of this large family from which many were to work the canal until its ending as a commercial waterway. Not all were canal boatmen, but were perhaps labourers or carters in canal-connected firms.

On the canal at Hest Bank

Setting the record straight

The reformer George Smith of Coalville in his scathing campaign of the lives of boat people said in 1873 *"To say that marriage is unknown among boatmen would be a libel, for more than half of them go through the legal ceremony and the remainder have a ceremony of their own."* suggesting that official marriage ceremonies did not always take place amongst *'boat people'*. The marriage registers in the churches of Preston. such as St John's, St Peter's, Holy Trinity and St Mark's reveals this not to be the case of the Lancaster Canal boat people, as almost all families have church baptism and marriage records. However, parents would sometimes wait until their travels brought them back to the *'home'* parish before having them baptised often resulting in several children of the same family being christened at the same ceremony.

Mary Ashcroft with father Tom Robinson (John Gavan)

Mary near Bellsfold Bridge (John Gavan)

Mary Robinson was born in 1914 at her grandmother's Preston home and brought with her parents, brothers and sisters on the Wigan Coal and Iron Company's boat *'Farewell'* and recalled, *"The seven of us would sleep in the cabin with Dad and Mother in one bed, two in the other bed place, one or two on the shelving and at least one of the lads on the floor. There were bigger families than ours living aboard at that*

24

time too." At the age of five she had to start her schooling in Preston and was boarded out. At weekends she went to a particular canal bridge at Preston and overturned a large stone. If her parents were to be in Preston on their boat then a message would be left. If not – *"back to the lodgings"*.

Mary and Dan began married life in 1931 on the horse barge *'May'* before switching to the Leeds & Liverpool carrying coal from Wigan to mills in Blackburn for *Dean Waddington's* on *'Edward'* This vessel, built at Riley Green in 1935 was named after the then Duke of Windsor. In the early nineteen thirties they moved to Baines's (ex Wigan Coal and Iron Company) vessel *'Express'* delivering coal to Cottam brickworks, Garstang gashouse, Storey's and Williamson's mills in Lancaster and the gas works at Carnforth and Kendal. Storey's had a huge tub on an overhead gantry and employed two coal heavers to discharge the vessel's cargo into this boat. At all other wharves, cargoes were off-loaded by barrow and shovel.

They wheeled their wheelbarrow
In an interview with Mike Taylor for *'Waterways World'* in 1987, Mary Ashcroft talked laughingly of the labourers who were the barrowers and shovellers. She spoke of tramps like *'Country Dick'*, *'Old Neversweat'*, *'Deaf Joe'* and *'Irish Johnny'* who used to help them *'barrow off'* at various places. *'Irish Johnny was a dirty old fellow. He had a big beard and always carried a large pack on his back. We used to let him sleep in our fore-cabin near the horse fodder and lock him in. He was alive with fleas and Dan once told me how Irish Johnny was jumping onto a boat, missed and fell in. He threw his pack onto the towpath and mice came leaping out of it in all directions. We were paid by trip, not tonnage. We usually carried 48 tons and if a boatman thought he'd been given too*

much, he'd shovel some overboard to help the horse, remembering where he'd dumped it so he could be 'kebbing' there if he was ever short' ("*Kebbing*" referred to using an iron rake to retrieve coal or other articles from the bottom of the canal.)

`Dan and Mary were a real '*team*', "*Dan used to lead the horse at Tewitfield Locks and I'd steer the boat in, catch the gate, climb up it and close it. He'd unhook the horse line from the swingletree* (a crossbar attached to the traces of a draft horse and to the vehicle or implement that the horse is pulling) *and stop the boat by hoisting the cloughs. Then he'd come and close the other gate and work one side of the lock while I did the other.*"

Dan said that the only way of making a living was a husband and wife partnership, "*two men not enough in it to make a wage each. Three pounds a journey for two of you and a horse, some weeks there would be two journeys, but some weeks only one.*"

Hincaster Tunnel was a tricky one to negotiate. Mary said that Dan would take a loaded boat through if the wind was against them but if there was a stern wind he'd perhaps say "*I think you can manage it today*" and it would be her turn to get down on a plank and "*leg it*" through while he took the horse over the top. ('*Legging*' was a method used to propel horse-drawn boats through tunnels which had no towing path, and the boatman had to push with his feet against the tunnel walls.) "*If it was a really strong stern wind, I could sometimes stay in the cabin and we'd get blown through*". Coming back empty they could perhaps push the boat through by hand, being careful of the slimy walls.

Dan spoke of an average working day of eighteen to twenty hours, sometimes working through the night until the following night to get a load on time. "*The wife and I could leave Preston with fifty tons at lunchtime today, unload at Lancaster tomorrow afternoon, thirty miles*

26

away. Back in Preston and load up again in the afternoon of the third day, sixty miles return."

The downward path

In the nineteen-forties trade began to decline. Dan recalled in a radio interview with Stewart Whaley of *'Radio Lancashire'* that when he started work in the early nineteen-twenties, there were forty six boats working, dwindling to four in 1947. The Ashcrofts had been delivering coal by boat to Kendal gasworks and Storey's of Lancaster but the very severe winter of 1946/47 when the canal was iced over meant that for three months the boats were stuck at Preston and could not be moved until April. During this time Storey's, who were the last firm on the canal to need coal delivered by boat, had switched to oil. The coal that was now surplus to requirements was unloaded and sold to a local hospital, as it was no longer the important commodity it had once been. This hailed the end of commercial traffic on the Lancaster canal. It was Joe Ashcroft who carried this final cargo in 1947.

Dan and Mary then moved to the Leeds-Liverpool in 1948, working again for *'Dean Waddingtons'* carrying coal to the paper mills at Blackburn. Eventually Dan left the canal and ran a coal merchant's business in Preston. The lure of the canal was still strong, however, as in 1949 he bgan the pleasure trips that continued for twenty five years.

Memories of a Canal Boatwoman - May Ashcroft (1923 – 2004)

May Sharp, nee Ashcroft was the daughter of Thomas Ashcroft and Fleetwood Hardman, and cousin of Dan. I talked to her two years before her death in 2004 and spent several hours with her and her husband John. Although her health was failing she was only too happy to talk about her childhood memories on the canal. Born in 1923 in Leighton Street, Preston near to the canal basin, the youngest of three sisters, she remembered with great affection the journeys from Preston to Lancaster and Kendal. They would depart from Preston basin fully loaded with 45 to 50 tons of coal. If the boat was filled to capacity it made it very hard for the horses to pull the

27

barge. The journey to Kendal loaded was around three days, while Lancaster took about one and a half. Accommodation was very limited in the boat but May recalls that it was very comfortable. Her parents slept in the stern and she remembers having to climb over their bed to get to her own before pulling the curtains round. Before settling for the night, the horse had to be stabled, fed and watered for the night.

When they arrived with their delivery of coal for Storey's Mill at Lancaster they would start to unload their cargo with the help of two men. May's mother would then give her a shopping list and she would take the

Thomas & Fleetwood Ashcroft

two-mile walk along the cutting into Penny Street in Lancaster. Her errands done she would set off to meet the boat for their return journey. So that she would know where to meet them, they left a piece of coal at a bridge along the way back and if there was no coal there May knew to wait for them. If they had a load for Kendal, they would stay overnight in Lancaster, stabling the horses. Other overnight stops included Bolton-le-Sands and Hest Bank from where they had a magnificent view over Morecambe Bay.

Out In all Weathers
Winter brought many hazards with snow and ice. May remembers being were frozen up for a month, waiting for the icebreaker as soon as the ice began to thaw and having to go to school in Carnforth. In 1936 a breach occurred at Nateby Hall when the banking collapsed, which meant that they were laid up for seventeen weeks whilst it was repaired.

Turning Their Hands to Other Things

The boatmen possessed many skills, not only in the expert handling of their crafts and care of their horses but also for their craftsmanship with rope. Thomas was renowned for his skill in making a *'turks head'* which was a thick plait of rope worked round the very top of the big wooden rudder to protect the paint. It was so called because it had the appearance of a turbaned Turk. Several *'turks heads'* often encircled the wooden tiller to save it from damaging the cabin roof. May remembered the Hincaster tunnel as being very dark and lonely and she had the responsibility of taking two horses along the narrow path over the top as her mother and father took the boat through the long dark tunnel. If, they were returning in that direction in the darkness with an empty boat, her father would take the horses himself, leaving May and her mother to take the boat through the tunnel. Here we see May (above) and Fleetwood on the tiller.

On The Seventh Day

In the nineteen thirties, boatmen were not permitted to use the locks on Sundays and one of May's jobs was to help her dad to work the locks in all weathers, sometimes in the dark with only a storm lamp. When the locks were empty they would stop overnight but sometimes if they wanted an early start they would set off in the early hours of Monday morning with a hand

Thomas, Fleetwood and May

lamp on the side of locks to guide them through. They would then go through the whole procedure of shutting the gates and filling up the locks. Working boatmen, especially on canals with a long flight of locks, would go on ahead to *set the locks in our favour* to save precious time in delivering their loads, a procedure which could cause problems for boats coming the other way.

The Hincaster now looks sad and neglected; the canal bed is dry and the vegetation overgrown. In 1980 the tunnel portals were restored by the 48th Field Squadron of the Royal Engineers, arranged by the Lancaster Canal Trust.

The waters around the beautiful area of Yealand Conyers and Crooklands were beautifully clear and unpolluted. The water tanks on the deck of the boat were filled on this stretch of the canal to provide drinking water. The area around the northern reaches was renowned for its farm produce - butter, eggs and the best bacon May reckoned she ever tasted. The watercress growing along the banks was regularly picked on the journey to be enjoyed later on.

Another of May's tasks every few weeks was to take the horse s to be shoed, which cost about twelve shillings in the 1930s. This meant crossing the A6 road to the blacksmith's forge and back. Horses could easily be frightened by a sudden noise. Once May was picking flowers and had to jump in the hedgerow. She could have jumped in the canal but unfortunately was no swimmer. The horse ran down the towpath but was eventually restrained by her father, who, like all bargees, was an accomplished horseman.

In 1939 at the age of sixteen her parents finally left the canal but found it hard to settle ashore. May soon adapted to her new life and enjoyed over sixty happy years of marriage with John. She died in August 2004 but her memories have been preserved with some of the photographs reproduced in this book which she took with a little *'Brownie'* camera.

Charles Ashcroft 1858 – 1910
Charles, one of the sons of Daniel and Elizabeth, was the great uncle of Dan and Joe, and my husband's great grandfather. This family connection with the canal came to an abrupt end when Charles died aged fifty one of cancer. Six years later, his son George, was killed in action on the Somme aged twenty eight and the entry in the *'Preston Roll of Honour'* states his occupation as 'bargeman'. The 1891 census shows Charles, his wife Mary Jane and sons George and William on the *'Albert'* at Forton.

A churchgoing family, Charles was a lay preacher in the *"Mission"* in Edward Street, a street where many of the Ashcroft family lived and part of which still survives. These *'chapels'* brought evangelical Christianity to poor areas, run by those who saw themselves as *'missionaries'*.

The Hampton Family

Many of the bargees on the canal worked for the larger boat companies such as *'Wigan Coal and Iron'*, *'Baines Brothers'* and *'Thompsons of Lancaster*. One family who owned several boats were the Hamptons. They were closely linked to the Ashcrofts; Joseph Hampton had married Ann Ashcroft, daughter of Daniel and Elizabeth in 1869 and on the 1881 census were on a canal boat at Winmarleigh Smithy bridge with Jane at the age of fifteen classed as *'the master's daughter, Assistant mate'*.

In 1885 Jane Hampton married Joshua Robinson, a coal merchant who later went on the canal when his coal business foundered. They were childless but brought up at least two other children, one of which was John Tickle who said about Jos: *"When I say mi dad, I'm referring to these people as mi parents. They weren't really, but to me they were. He were a real quiet man, a real gent, quiet with' horses, quiet wi t' boat. Everything had to be right, and if a horse hadn't done well, it hadn't to be punished. He would say, he needs a rest or a change in his feed. Real grand fella, nothing were too much trouble for him. He would not see anybody stuck, if he saw a man and his wife and he had no discharger, he would help them out, he could always catch up his time again."*

Jos worked for his brother in law Jim Hampton for a short time on his three boats, *'Venture'*, *'Clara'* and *'Harold'*. John says *"I don't think he wanted to work for a relation and it was different way of boating to what he wanted. There was not the variety, just the short trips.*

A Fearful Day

Jim had married a *"factory girl"* called Nellie, though John said *"she were a real boatwoman."* Jim told him about a hair-raising trip to Glasson on a very windy day, about 1919. The wind was an enemy of the boat, and it was a fight against the elements on the way down, with the wind coming down from the sea. *"A fearful day."* Nellie was steering the boat whilst Jim went to set the locks on his bike. Not only had Nellie to manage the lock gates on her own, if Jim had not got back from setting the next ones, she had to set the horse off as the lock gates opened. From the locks they had to go across the big basin to the ship for their load. Jim set off with the horses down through the basin gradually losing control of the boat. Nearly across the basin, the wind seized the boat, landing broadside on and the horses could no longer control it. Jim had to cut the hauling line, and told Nellie to get down in the boat or go in the cabin. The horses were then cut loose, to stop them going under the water. The boat went across broadside and landed under trees at the other side where it was soft mud. After tying the horses up to the warehouse, and checking to see if Nellie was all right, the horses were then taken to the stables at the *'Victoria'* for the night. John says of Jim *"If he hadn't been a boatman with a really good knife, he could have lost two horses."*

Company Policy

Jos worked for his brother in law Jim Hampton for a short time on his three boats, *'Venture'*, *'Clara'* and *'Harold'*. The *'Venture'* was one of the oldest canal boats passed down from Jim's father" *"old Joe Hampton"*. Old Joe was always whittling away with a knife and his John Tickle remembers him making a model of the *'Venture'* in perfect detail.

The three Hampton boats were mostly run by the family and John says about working for them *"We were always making good money on Hamptons. Normal pay was two shillings a mile and nothing for running empty. Two men could make a good living out of it."*

They were mostly short trips, from Preston to Stone Chimney Coal yard, Catforth, or Woodplumpton, Glasson was a regular trip and occasionally Carnforth or Priest Hutton.

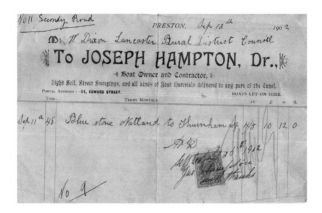

Where there's muck
Another regular job was taking all the street sweepings out of Preston which were taken out of the 'muck fields' at the top of Marsh Lane, after it had been tipped in by a horse and cart, then loaded into the boat and taken to different wharves up and down the canal for farmers. At this time, streets were full of horse muck because traffic was mostly horse-drawn.

A grand old cock
John's 'grandad', old Joe Hampton, was *'a real character'*, who used to point to the weathervane on the steeple of St Walburge's church, Preston and say *"I've stood on that stone"*. Joe claimed to have carted the stone and stood on it when it was loaded on the boat bottom.

The Needham and Walmsley families
One of the few boatmen who originated from the northern part of the canal was Aquila Needham, born in Tewitfield in 1850. His wife Hannah Walmsley was the sister of Mary, wife of Thomas Baines. In the winter of 1884 tragedy struck when Aquila died of

34

pneumonia following a fall into the canal, leaving a wife and three children. In 1881 census the family were moored at Ellel, their only son Joseph lodging with his uncle Joseph Walmsley in Ladywell Street, Preston. In 1891, they were at 5 Nixon's Row, just off Ladywell Street and Hannah is classed on the census as *'a widow living on her own means'* and Joseph her son now aged 19, is *'a hay and straw dealer.* Quil Calland,* Aquila's grandson tells of his grandmother setting up Joe in a *'flourishing'* hay and straw provender business and how every Thursday, on his half day from work he would deliver hay and provender to various customers by horse and cart. The list of businesses in Marsh Lane in the Ordnance Survey Map of Preston North dated 1909 states: *"Needham J., hay and c., dealer"* and the name of *"Joseph Needham, provender dealer,"* appears in the Barrett's trade directory of Preston and District for 1932.

Land-based canal connections

Aquila and Hannah's youngest daughter Ann eventually took over the canal boat business, owning seven barges and the story was that she was the first woman to navigate a canal boat from the Preston to Lancaster canal to the Leeds and Liverpool via the Glasson arm and the sea. This would have been a very tricky manoeuvre for anyone and would have been very unusual for a woman to attempt. She sold the boats to a Baines cousin, who was probably Lawrence Baines, immediately doubling their fleet. It is not clear what year Ann gave up the boats but in 1909 at the age of twenty five she married Thurston Calland, stating her occupation as *'cotton winder'.*

Shuttleworth and son, lock-keepers

John Shuttleworth was a lock-keeper on the seven Tewitfield Locks, from the 1920s to around 1946/7. He originated from Over Kellet working in Carnforth Coal Yard and when he got the job at Tewitfield he moved all his family and household belongings up the canal to Tewitfield in a barge. His son Edmund took over when he retired and remained there until Top Lock Cottage was demolished in 1963 to make way for the M6. He then moved to the Canal Keeper's Cottage at Crooklands.

Top Lock Cottage, Tewitfield

Photographs courtesy of Mark Shuttleworth, great, great grandson of John.

AN OLD REPROBATE'S MEMORIES: JOHN PARKINSON

John Parkinson was born in 1934 at No 10 Mill Hill, Preston. This house was rented for 4/6d a week complete with stables, essential for a boatman as in 1930 stabling was at a premium in Preston town centre. His canal pedigree goes back several generations on both sides with connections to the Robinsons, Ashcrofts, Fazackerleys, Knowles and Vickers. His grandfather John's second marriage was to Margaret Cross, nee Ashcroft, a widow with two sons, Richard and Abraham. *('Abe'* Cross was a boatman that John Tickle worked for occasionally helping to unload cargo helping to unload cargo at Ratcliffe Wharf, near Forton.) John attended St Peter's school near the canal basin and at the start of each trip to Lancaster or Kendal, his mother would take him there whilst his father was preparing the boat and horse.

The family in 1934 lived on the boat *'Ann'* but at the time of John's birth, was under repair so he was born on dry land. Shortly after, his parents, Ernest and Ada, took the *'Express'* with his aunt Agnes.

'Express' at Preston Basin c 1923

``Let's Be Off"

When the boatmen had finished loading the boats, before he could set off, there would be a visit from the *'School Board'* for the children, and the *'Humane officer'* for the animals. His mother would go shopping for groceries, visiting either *'McConachies'* on Fylde Road or *'Nellie Ashcrofts.'* who were both convenient for the canal basin. In those days shops used a *'slate'* system (i.e. credit) but as the boatman and his family could be away for two weeks or more, they would settle up before they left, or pay so much off their bill. A list would be left of what she needed and John remembers *'old Abe Ashcroft'* in his brown smock and wickerwork basket, coming down to the boat before they set off with the order. Then she would perhaps call at *'Preston Farmers'* in Lune Street for provender supplies. Another visit she had to make was to go and *'sign on'* at the Employment Exchange, They would give her a postcard and just before departure at lunchtime, her employer (probably one of the Baines brothers) filled it in, put a stamp on it and she would be eligible for half a days *'dole'* i.e. unemployment pay. When she returned to Preston and the boat was tied up, perhaps waiting for cargo or it was summertime and trade slack, she would possibly get three days on the dole.

The principal customers for the cargoes were the gasworks at Kendal, Carnforth and Garstang and Storey's of Lancaster, who took about eleven barge-loads per week, discharging two per day, one on Saturday, none on Sunday. On Monday night the horses were put in the stables at Mill Hill and next morning whilst his father was waiting his turn to load, a visit may have been made to the blacksmith in Pitt Street. By the time they arrived at the bottom of the basin, mother had returned and great uncle Bob might be there, helping with the hauling line. Great uncle Bob was Robert Ashcroft, and was nicknamed *'Dandy Bob'*. He cut a fine figure with his apparel, his *'ganzy'*, (woollen jersey) cord trousers and *'dandy'* clogs (highly polished, fancy) complete with pearl buttons. He was renowned for his clog dancing, playing the concertina and spoons, and could *"tell a good story"*. Another nickname for him was *'latchlifter'* so called as he was famous for only ever having enough money for two pints of beer (enough to *'lift the latch'* at the pub.) Then he would rely on his repartee of stories to keep the offers of beer flowing.

Just before sailing, the boatman had to replenish the water supplies mostly at Durham's coalyard, being one of the few places with a tap. He would take his buckets and fill the water tank to the brim - twenty gallons.   Some would be set aside for drinking water. Travelling north the water in the canal was pure enough to use.   A horse trough was situated where the *'Watering Trough'* public house still stands in Fylde Road but as the horses preferred to drink from the canal, the trough was mostly unused and later removed.

Taking his turn along with the other bargees, the boat would be loaded from the railway wagons which had brought coal or coke from Wigan.   By the time they arrived at the bottom of the basin, mother had returned and they were ready to go.   Once they left the starting place, the boatman would stay on the bank with the horses as they could be distracted by traffic noise. His wife would be at the tiller.   Then uncle Bob would take over the horses and dad would go to the *'pie shop'*.

The traffic noise at Lane Ends Bridge in Preston sometimes made the horses *'skittish'* but as they passed through, they would settle down, dad would get aboard and take over the steering.   Pies would be eaten on the move, and the cabin would be thoroughly cleaned.   By now they were at a steady pace, two and a quarter m.p.h (two and a half in good water).   As they were approaching 'four milestone' the horse's feed would be prepared   They would also be looking out for craft coming the other way, as at that time of day, craft would have discharged at Lancaster early morning and be on their way back.

The rule of the Preston to Kendal canal :
'Vessels proceeding from the Preston end of the canal will keep to the towing path side and will not cease to haul. Vessels proceeding from the south will proceed to the other side and drop their tow rope as they pass.'
'unless the vessel proceeding from Preston to Kendal is empty.'
When the boats used to pass each other there was a surprising amount of information that passed between them. *""What's on at pictures?" Have you seen so and so?"*

Whipcrack away
As they approached bridges or other places where visibility was poor, a means of warning others coming the other way was set down in byelaws which the boatman had to be familiar with:
"Each vessel's skipper to provide an audible means of warning". On horse drawn vessels the audible method of warning was the whip which would be six or seven feet long. Most of the women used the *'side whip'*, the men the *'overhead'* one. As John's mother was only 4 ft 10 inches tall and the whip six feet in length, she walked to the side of the vessel, usually starboard, leaned on the tiller and would crack the whip *'cowboy style'*. One crack was all it took. They then went on the bank, listening for someone cracking on the other side of the bridge. You then gave a series of two cracks. That meant as they were coming from Preston they had the right of way. If you heard a crack from the other side of the bridge, that meant they'd stopped and you sailed. The whip was also used if they wanted to warn someone of their intention to change sides, or were agreeable to the one on the other side wanting to do likewise, they would raise their whip in their right hand, the other one would see it and raise it.

Boatmen often sailed *'in company'* with their relatives. John remembers great uncle Joe Ashcroft and his son Sam sailing with them and sometimes great aunt Nancy would come to help with the locks at Tewitfield. They would repeat the feeding of the horses just beyond the *'nine milestone'*, at Hollowforth where there was one of only three swing bridges on the Lancaster. There was a stable in a farmyard and the horses would sense their presence, but if they were busy eating they would carry on as normal. They would keep going, John perhaps walking on the bank with the horses, reaching Stubbins at Catterall, at about six or seven o'clock in the evening, a journey of fifteen miles. The horses would be stabled and dad and Uncle Sam would go on their bicycles to the *'Kenlis Arms.'*. Wednesday they would travel by the same routine, horses fed every four miles, cabin cleaned and meals eaten on the way.

'Snuff said about old rope

Approaching Lancaster, John's dad who often used to walk around with bits of rope round his neck would slice it into lengths and put in a bag, ready to sell in Lancaster. Whenever the boatman got a new rope, the old one was cut up for sale. Mother walked into the city from Penny Street Bridge for any supplies that were needed, sometimes meeting *'Aunt Nancy'* who had come by train from Preston. On their way down, farmers would say *"Fetch us two of Number One and a threepenny special"*. The coal heavers employed by Ernest would get snuff from Kendal and Aunt Nancy and her husband Joe, along with many others, were partial to a pinch of snuff.

John particularly remembers the pungent aroma of *'Wilson's No 1'* which was in a tin. The user would take a pinch from the tin with his/her thumb and finger, deposit it on the back of the other hand, then sniff it up into the nostrils. In the meantime their boat would perhaps discharge at Storey's Mill, where coal heavers or men wishing to buy rope would be waiting. A chap called Joe Slater used to turn up to buy *'cow ties'* (a short length of rope) to later sell at the auction mart.

There were characters amongst the coal heavers. *'Old Neversweat'*, and *'Watercress Dick'* were two of them. The latter was so named because of his special *'trade'*. He was employed on a casual basis at Lancaster to discharge vessels but he would have risen very early, caught the early bus and along with his wickerwork basket would pick watercress from the banks of the canal (the type of watercress

41

which is now known as *'rocket'*). He would bundle it up and sell it in Lancaster later.

Before the 1930s Education Acts, children had traditionally helped to unload cargoes but this was now considered, especially in large towns like Kendal as *'child labour'* so boatmen would employ perhaps two men to discharge coal into the gas works, paying them 7/6d each. In 1936, the rate to discharge a load of coal was 22 shillings 6d. Most of the utilities or mills the *'consignee'* would pay the discharge money direct to the boatmen who would pay his *'employees'* (the coal heavers).

Up with the Thursday lark
Thursday was a morning John had to be up especially early for an *'early start'* as he was expected to help with the eight locks at Tewitfield. He had particular jobs to do even as a small child and as he grew up he could walk down with the horse and follow the boat to the next lock and help to open and close gates. He was taught to steer, usually when they were going down with a *'light,,* i.e. empty, boat.

They would arrive at Kendal Thursday evening. The gasworks had lighting so it was then possible to work into the night and complete the discharge on Friday morning. On Friday they would sail back to Tewitfield and stay there overnight. Saturday morning up bright and early again. Off to Carnforth to load stone for Lancaster.

On the seventh day
On certain canals, Sunday working was not allowed or positively discouraged. Uncle George Proctor (brother of John's grandmother, Alice Parkinson) was a sidesman at St Thomas's Church, Garstang, not far from the canal, and often tried to stop the boat sailing through the town on a Sunday morning. John's granddad and father would time their sailings for when the service was well under way, as Uncle George would be *'concentrating on his collection plate'*.

 This was not the first time that Grandad John Parkinson had been *'at the wrath'* of Uncle George. He often came to the churchyard to tend his wife's grave and Uncle George had told the vicar that grandad was a *'reprobate in this parish and every parish along the canal side, neither let or tithe'*, meaning he didn't pay tithe to the church or rent a property. Prior to the canal being built in 1790 the inhabitants of the small outlying villages and hamlets along its way rarely moved from one area to another. Once the boatman came to work the canal he was looked upon as an interloper and as long as he kept to the canal corridor without stopping didn't stop they were happy. John Parkinson says *"they were tarred with the same brush as the banditi (navvies) what dug it"*.

Leaving Garstang they would probably sail back in the company of Uncle Joe, heading for Hollowforth on the outskirts of Barton to be ready for discharging Monday morning, using labourers from Moon's Farm to discharge the boats. Running to Kendal, on a Sunday the family used to tie up for Sunday dinner, his mother having been to the butchers at Carnforth for a nice piece of brisket. They all looked forward to the one meal where they were not on the move. Boatmen and women alike would go to the *'Kenlis Arms'* for a few pints then return to the boat and sit down together. The canteen of cutlery would have been brought out for this special occasion and John remembers relatives who lived in Preston coming out and sailing back home on the boats. Monday meant return to Preston for discharging; the end of a full week's trip.

Towards the end
As trade declined boatmen got work on Preston docks or as carters. Ernest Parkinson sometimes carted bricks to *'Cottam Tile & Brick Company.'* Lack of trade at the start of the Second World War meant that the docks could no longer absorb the boatmen and a decision was made by John's parents to move over to the Leeds-Liverpool canal. Ernest had had brief spells working for Dean Waddingtons on that canal, along with Dan Ashcroft but had always gone back to

the Lancaster. However, in 1941 they decided to move 'lock stock and barrel' to the Leeds-Liverpool Canal and that is how John came to be living, as he still does, at Blackrod.

Another factor that prompted their decision was that John's mother, Ada was expecting a baby and a permanent address would ensure she received regular treatment for her confinement. John spent the rest of his working life on the boats but on far busier canals such as the Leeds-Liverpool and the Bridgewater. The title of 'th'owd reprobate' has been passed on to him.

A detailed account of his childhood and working life is preserved in the North West Sound Archive at Clitheroe Castle, available to the public.

CANAL LIFE

The Lancaster boat comes sailing,
We watch as it goes past.
Starting on a journey
Up the cut to Kendal Gas.
The woman at the tiller
Guides them deftly through.
The boatman and his family
Are skipper, mate and crew.
The days are lone and sometimes tough
For the boatman and his wife.
A world apart – a waterway,
Their home, their job, their life.

(John Parkinson)

Postcard of 'Beehive' at Myerscough with Roebuck public house on far right

Garstang Wharf (The Waterways Trust/The Boat Museum)

Broken Back Bridge Lancaster

THE LANCASTER CANAL BOAT

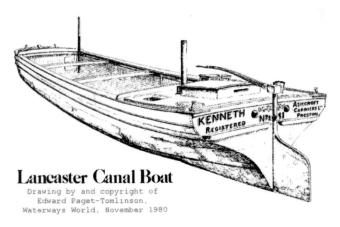

Lancaster Canal Boat
Drawing by and copyright of
Edward Paget-Tomlinson,
Waterways World, November 1980

Lancaster canal boats were 14 ft. 6 in wide and 72 ft. long with a maximum capacity of 52 tons and always horse-drawn, sometimes by two horses. They had square sterns and latterly were built of steel by W Allsupp & Sons, Preston, then towed round to the canal at Glasson Dock via the River Ribble and the sea. Some were partly built on Preston Docks, brought up Marsh Lane and launched into the canal to be fitted out. Square sterns were ideal for coal boats as they accommodated more cargo.

As the Lancaster canal was shallower than the Leeds-Liverpool canal, it meant that 'Lanky' boats had a shallower draft and smaller load carrying capacity. Those boats which carried bulk cargoes, such as coal or limestone, did not have side decks or any way of covering the cargo to protect it from the weather. Most of the cargoes of grain, which would need weather protection, would have been taken by rail after completion of the Lancaster and Preston Railway in 1840 and the Glasson Dock branch railway in 1883.

Wooden boats needed more repair and facilities were few on this canal so they died out in the late nineteenth century. John Brockbank, a shipyard owner from Lancaster built some of the earlier ones and on 28th August 1793 launched an earth-carrying boat at Ellel which was probably the first boat on the Lancaster canal. His cargo boats *'Bee'* and *'Ceres'* carried the Lancaster canal committee and their friends when the canal opened on 22nd November 1797 whilst *'Elephant'* carried other canal owners. Yet another of his boats, *'Ant'* carried a load of coal and cannel to the opening ceremony. Other boats that he built were *'Cragg'* in March 1800 and *'Rob Roy'* completed in 1819, both commissioned by the Earl of Balcarres, a major Wigan coalmines owner. As early as 1825 he had boats on the Lancaster Canal as follows:-

"Zara"	valued at £100	*"Garstang"*	valued at £300
"Neptune"	valued at £100	*"Dandy"*	valued at £290
"Petronius"	valued at £230	*"Rob Roy"*	valued at £220
"Preston"	valued at £235	*"Dick"*	valued at £220
"Thomas"	valued at £70	*"Eolus"*	valued at £100
"Glasgow"	valued at £260	*"Bobby Friend"*	valued at £300

Stars and roundels

In *"Canal and River Craft"*, Edward Paget-Tomlinson describes the distinctive decorations of the Lancaster canal boats. *"Boats were decorative in the old days, with scroll work on the square stern but later Lancaster boatmen favoured stars and roundels and the name in large letters across the stern. One of the principal carriers, the Wigan Coal and Iron Co. had red-sterned boats with rows of white five-pointed stars along the gunwale and across the stern, while Baines Brothers with their buff-coloured sterns, had a dot/dash decoration in black and yellow along the gunwale at the fore end".*

Most photographs of Lancaster barges were rear views to show the vessel name, owner and registration details. In a rare front view, *'Redwing'* is seen at Cottam Hall, just outside Preston, in about 1910. The horse is being led by Dan Ashcroft senior. The patterns on the bow indicate that the vessel was owned at the time by Thompsons of Lancaster.

 The cabin of the Lancaster canal boat was approximately fourteen feet wide and sixteen feet in length. There was a double bed right across the stern and up the other side of the boat, offside, on the opposite side to the doorway, called the side bed, which was a narrow one like a single bed. The bed space was divided up by use of bed boards, relevant to the size of the boatman's family. There was room at one end for storage and a fireplace in the middle right against the bulk head and on the side of the boat a form, to sit on with drawers under it, as a means of utilising available space. There were also cupboards to store groceries and pots, and a little curtained alcove, where the *'chamber pot'* or *'guzunder'* was placed. This would be later emptied into a *'midden'* (a heap of dung or refuse,) sometimes referred to as a *'dunghill*, on the way.

One of the main cargoes in Preston was manure in the late 1800s, so to comply with Public Health Acts a false *'bulkhead'* was put in away from cabin accommodation. As they built the iron vessels it meant the cabin was appreciably bigger than the original wooden ones, the manure trade having declined by this time.

In the *'forecastle'* or *'fo'c'sle'* situated in the bow of the boat was storage for the horses's harness, provender and hay. There was also a bench with a small hand turned machine for chopping hay which was then bagged and mixed with other provender to feed the horses. Hay would have been picked up on the way, netted and put into a stable at Lancaster for future use. The rest was brought down to the stabling rented by the boatmen.

'Bare Boat Charter'

A boatman who was contracted to one of the main carriers like Wigan Coal and Iron Co. was mostly *'self employed'* on what was known as a *'bare boat charter'* Taking over a boat for the first time, it would only be fitted with the items laid down by the Canal Boat Acts. These were the twenty gallon water tanks on deck, the stove and certain bed places. The rest of his equipment such as towing masts, ropes, provender and his horses had to be provided by the boatman himself. Under Ministry of Labour Acts, out of his wages he was allotted one third for the upkeep and maintenance of his horses, the remaining two thirds were used for general living costs and for paying wages and discharging money. Other equipment integral to the job were planks, barrows and spades.

The Up and Coming Thing

Towards the end of the First World War, two steam powered vessels *'Asland'* and *'Cricket'* were brought off the Leeds-Liverpool canal for a trial period by Thompson's of Lancaster. The steamers were intended to pull four boats mostly to Ratcliffe Wharf near Cockerham and to White Cross and the Electrical Works at Lancaster and would replace the horses. The *'Cricket'* had been known by other names, *'Pioneer'* when owned by Dean Waddington of Blackburn but was later known as *'Progress'* when owned by T G W Wells of Wigan. John Parkinson remembers the boat still working when he left school about 1948.

The main traders joined in the *'towage'* system, cutting the boatmen's wage rate by one third, as he would not have the expense of keeping a horse. It was not a success on this canal. True there were no horses to be attended to but as winter came and the canal began to freeze there were problems with the ice cutting the bow of the wood boats. Losing trade, Thompson's tried to remedy this by having tin plates put round the boat but the ice even took the plates off and they were frozen up again. Even more problems were encountered at Tewitfield locks as the boats had to be pulled in the lock one at a time and by the time the steamer had arrived at the bottom of eight locks, he then had to wait until the last vessel came up that lock. As they had no horse, the only way of getting up the locks was by "bow hauling" (the men pulling the boat by the towrope). A horse was hired from the local farmer but again proved so time consuming that it was considered impractical.

A square sterned steamer, the *'Clara'* owned by S R Thompson's ran from Glasson Dock to Lancaster in the nineteen twenties, and was later sold to Hampton's. It was unsuccessful as it lacked sufficient power. Soon after they reverted back to horses, but the boatman never regained the third of his wage that he had lost.

The Maintenance Boats
'Bank rangers' looked after the canal banks and the dredging boat helped to keep the weeds down. They were responsible for a length of about seven miles of canal, living in a provided house. The bank ranger's boat was referred to as a *'muck boat'*, an oblong boat with a flat front. All the boatmen used to allow them a bit of coal off the boat to keep their fire going. It was never handed to them but as the boat was sailing past a bucketful of coal or *'slack'* was left on the bank. As a boatman said, *"It did a bit of good keeping on the right side of the bank rangers".*

Bank rangers' boat at Wyre Aqueduct

They usually worked in teams and their duties were varied, they would go along the canal doing repairs, helping to mend breaches, looked for leaks, mowed hay and made their own gates. Two of the Canal Company's boats used by the bank rangers were the *'Olive'* and the *'Stella'*.

Hilda Robinson's father, William Bewes, was a canal bank ranger for thirty years from 1923 to 1954 and lived in *'Belmont Cottage'*, Hest Bank where Hilda was born in 1925. The boatmen used to moor overnight to rest the horses and the families came to listen to William and Isabel's gramophone. Belmont Cottage, long since demolished had stables at one end, a large wash-house in the centre and living accommodation at the other end. There was a living room and kitchen on the ground floor, two bedrooms on the first floor and a large attic on the second. There were also two large cellars and hay lofts over the stables. There was no running water or electricity so they used paraffin lamps and water from a well in the field behind the cottage. The water flowed into *'Saint Patrick's Well'* reputed to be holy water and people were known to collect this water to cure eye ailments.

In 1953 Hilda's parents went to live at *'Aqueduct Cottage'*, which was situated immediately north of Halton Road bridge, Lancaster. This cottage too has been demolished. William was then in charge of the length from *'Deep Cutting'*, which ran from *Haverbreaks* to Carnforth.

William and Isabel with daughter Hilda

As well as his bank ranger's duties William also used to help with haymaking at a local farm. Another job was to occasionally fish bodies out of the canal, not a very pleasant one but he was paid a shilling for each body, probably by the coroner or police. Hilda remembers as a child an inquest into a drowning being held in *'Belmont Cottage'* from which she was ushered quickly away.

Cargoes

Besides coal and limestone, one of the cargoes integral to the canal trade was manure. During the 1840's when the Canal Company took over the railways they realised that money could be made by selling manure to farmers along the canal. The Whitsuntide Walks in Preston were known in the trade as *'Muck Monday'* and were lucrative both to the Company and the boatmen, because of the horses used in the processions.

Round about February each year the Canal Company would send their boat along and load the manure taken from the eleven stables they owned. This would then be loaded up and sold and a profit made. A portion of this money would be paid out to the boatmen who rented their stables, usually on the Saturday before Whit Monday. This agreement meant that the boatman had *'brokered a deal with the canal company'* to allow him to stable his horses. This *'windfall'* would mean the boatmen could have a good *'booze up'* in one of the town centre public houses over the Whitsuntide period.

One of the main trades prior to 1900 was that of the transportation of night soil. During the year horse manure would be collected and put onto the *'muck field'* which was at the end of Kendall Street, Preston. It was tipped into vessels overnight at the bottom of Edward Street to be taken away and would then be discharged into a field or different brickcrofts several miles out of the town. The firm of Hampton's used to specialise in this type of work and some of their men were contracted to spread it on the land for use by the farmers.

The main Preston Docks called *'Ashton Dock'* used to be situated on Strand Road and it enabled cargo to be transhipped to Ashton Basin and then onto the canal. Commodities like potatoes were brought in from Ireland and taken to Glasson Dock. The Glasson branch was built in 1826 to the Port of Glasson on the River Lune, allowing the speedier import and export of raw materials. Sea-going barges could offload their cargoes onto barges instead of sailing to Lancaster on the Lune. It was also possible for small coasting craft to come directly onto the canal. On 16 May that year a sloop called 'Sprightly' reached Preston from the Duddon estuary with a cargo of Cumberland slate, the first boat to sail on the canal from Glasson Dock to Preston. The first vessel built and launched at Glasson was a 'superior sort of canal boat' called the 'Acorn', a boat 70 feet long and 14 feet broad. The Glasson Dock Arm of the canal runs from Lodge Hill, near Galgate to Glasson Dock, it is two and a half miles long and has a flight of six locks plus the sea-lock. At the junction with the main line is a lock-keeper's cottage and a turnover bridge crossing the arm.

Drawing by Tony Lewery

Oats were taken along the canal to Woodplumpton, Salwick and Lancaster to the watermills and windmills there. Animal hides were carried into Lancaster or Preston to be bought and sold at the cattle auctions.

Dan Ashcroft said that his main cargoes were hardcore, industrial fuel, slack, (coal dust) and road material. Another cargo was timber carried from Kendal which went mostly up to Gatebeck Gunpowder works at Sedgwick to be sawn up to make boxes for the gunpowder. One of the most unusual cargoes was that of bulrushes which on certain parts of the canal grew in abundance. They would be scythed down and put in bundles ready to be used by the Catholic churches in Preston to make crosses for Palm Sunday.

Decline of the Working Boats

In 1926, the year of the General Strike, according to the canal boat inspection book, *"canal work came to a complete standstill, beyond an occasional boat ladened with sand or road material, as coal transport will probably form 95 per cent of the total canal traffic."* During this year of the miners' strike, coal was collected from Polish ships in Glasson Dock. During the First World War, to keep the boatmen on the canal systems, they had been given *'war bonuses'* so as to tempt them away from more lucrative jobs on munitions.

Miners' strikes in 1913 adversely affected the coal trade and in the nineteen twenties many mineowners had amalgamated, such as Wiigan Iron & Coal Company now formed part of *'Lancashire Associated Collieries'* and struck a deal with the railways to put coal on railway sidings, put in bags and sell direct to the public, instead of delivering coal by barge. They went out of business in 1928. Other coal dealers, such as S R Thompson and W I Turner of Lancaster lasted until 1932 on the canal but W I Turner was still dealing in coal in 1960.

The Baines Brothers bought boats from these firms at a reasonable rate, plus the vessels of the Hamptons. By the nineteen thirties, the number of working boats on the Lancaster was declining and in 1933 only five families were crewing eleven boats.

List of Registered Boats and Masters on 24 January 1933

"Express"	Thomas Parkinson	*"Joseph"*	Tied up
"Wegber"	R Ashcroft	*"James"*	R Cross
"Iron Duke"	Tied up	*"Farewell"*	Tom Robinson
"Clara"	Tied up	*"Benjamin"*	J Ashcroft
"Richard"	Tied up	*"Sarah"*	James Robinson
"Kendal"	Tied up	*"Ann"*	Mrs Robinson
"Harold"	James Hampton	*"Prince*	A Thackeray
"May"	Dan Ashcroft	*of Wales"*	

The 1891 census shows that twenty seven boats were in operation, crewed by twenty four families but does not take into account those that were out of commission at the time. No canal boat registration books are available, apart from the years 1929 to 1938 on this waterway. In 1907, thirty three barges were on the canal but six of these were laid up. By 1916 twenty five boats remained working, five having been broken up since 1907. From this time no new boats were brought on to the canal. By 1931 the total number was down to 15. In the 1870s a total of 55 boats were registered and working the canal, the highest recorded.

At the start of the Second World War, the main customers on the canal were the three gas works at Kendal, Carnforth and Lancaster. The introduction in wartime of a *'blackout'* system, meant less demand for fuel by the utilities, so the boatman lost a large percentage of his trade. A further blow was the formation of the Ministries of Food and Power, which declared that anywhere north of the River Lune had to be supplied by Cumbria or Yorkshire collieries. This also took a large percentage of business and made many boatmen *'surplus.'* The docks at Preston, which had traditionally found work for the boatmen in slack periods were also suffering a decline due to wartime restrictions, which included the cutting off of the cattle trade from Northern Ireland.

'Redwing' at Aldcliffe Boat House (Lancaster Maritime Museum)

'Herbert' under ownership of S Kent (Percy Duff Collection)

An article in the *'Preston Herald'* in 1944 headed *"The Romance of a Derelict Waterway"* by J H Spencer paints a bleak picture of even further decline and neglect in the Preston area of the canal. He wrote:- *"These long reaches of the canal have now become a fen of stagnant waters. As seen from the Marsh Lane bridge, the prospect is one of silent spaciousness with idle travelling cranes across the canal, and where was once a hive of human activity is now practically deserted. Traffic on the canal has almost ceased, at most there are only at the present time, six canal boats working and a few days ago I saw two of these under repair, the "Wasp" and the "Ann". The very names of the boats give colour to the halcyon days of yore when these barges were decorated in gay colours of red and yellow on a black background."* When the waterways were nationalised in 1947, boats were even less colourful, painted in a livery of blue and yellow in a blundering attempt to impose some sort of uniformity on the national waterways system.

Mr Spencer continued *"I am told there is difficulty in getting bargemen today, many of the older men have died and there is no encouragement offered to younger men to take on this job, being no hope of continuity of employment."* This of course was 1944, the year when the boats were sold to the existing bargees who failed to *"make a go"* of operating their barges, faced with competition from rail and road. Mr Spencer's words were proved to be prophetic. He suggested the solution could be introducing motor boats on the canal but admits that *"these would not be suitable for the canal in its present state, the banks are not strong enough to withstand the wash they cause and to make them more durable would entail heavy expenditure".*

What fate awaited?

By the mid- nineteen thirties *'Charles', 'Joseph', 'Iron Duke', 'Robert' ,'Kendal'. 'Wegber, 'James' 'Richard' 'Clara' and 'Venture'* had all been dismantled. The last canal boats to be registered in Preston were *'Kenneth', 'Herbert', 'Wasp', 'Benjamin' and 'Ann'* and the registration of all these boats was surrendered in March 1948 under the name of Ashcroft Canal Carriers Ltd. which had been formed by Daniel Ashcroft senior in 1942 along with his three sons who continued to take coal to canal-side mills in Lancaster until the mills switched to oil in 1947.

"*Benjamin*", (shown right) which was the boat Charles Ashcroft was crewing in 1882, was sold to a firm at Hest Bank for use as a floating office. It didn't last long and the boat was sunk in the basin by the Lune Aqueduct, later cut up and removed. *'Kenneth' and 'Ann'* were also both sunk at Preston Basin, which was later in filled and a new British Rail office built over them. *'Herbert'* finished its days as a landing stage at Peel on the Isle of Man. *'Harold'* and *'Wasp'* suffered the same destiny as most of the others, being sunk then cut up and removed.

The Last of the Line

The *'Lady Fiona'*, launched in 1873 is the last Lancaster *"wide beam"* canal boat in existence. Originally named *'Pet'* the boat was owned by the Lancaster Canal Company and described by it as the *'Fylde Market Boat'*.

'Pet's' last cargo was coal to the mills in Lancaster in 1946 and then used as a maintenance boat, changing her name to the *"Lady Moira"*. *She was possibly used as a 'spoon dredger,* a primitive type of dredger consisting of large wooden or iron spoons mounted on a boat or flat and used for scooping mud from the bottom of a canal or waterway and also served as an icebreaker. In 1956 Jack Ellison converted the boat to carrying passengers and renamed her *'Lady Fiona'*, after his granddaughter, who was aged eleven at the time. She operated until 2003 when the owner decided the cost of bringing her up to modern standards could not be justified and put her on the market.

She is now (2006) part of a £75,000 project for restoration by British Waterways and upon completion will be used as an educational resource.

'Pet' at Penny Street Bridge c 1895 (Lancaster Maritime Museum)

'Pet' c 1960 in use as a maintenance boat (John Parkinson)

THE CANAL BOAT INSPECTOR CALLS

The passing of the *'Canal Boats Acts'* 1877 and 1884 required all vessels with living accommodation to register with the local authority and to undergo regular inspections by Sanitary Inspectors. (The registers for 1929 to 1938 for the Lancaster canal are held in the Lancashire Record Office, Preston).

These Acts were passed to prevent overcrowding of families on boats. A look at the census of 1861 shows quite large families and sometimes crew members living on board. The *'Clyde'* in Preston basin had on board Thomas Iddon and his family, a total of twelve persons. At Glasson Dock that same year there were two boats, the *'Supply'* with Thomas Fawcett and wife and seven children, and *'Eliza'* with Thomas Parkinson, wife Winifred and six children. The largest family on the 1881 census was the Churchhouses on *'Pet'* tied up at Ellel. James and Margaret (nee Hampton) had eight children.

The *'Annual Report of the 'Inspector of Health'*, for Lancaster, shows that in 1920 the number of boats inspected was 21. Living on board were 24 adult males, 10 adult females and eight children. He said:- *"There is good health, no sickness of any sort being seen amongst them despite the harsh rough life they follow."* This is hardly surprising as conditions for workers in the town in the cotton mills were working ten hour days, six days a week, without the benefit of the fresh air enjoyed by the canal families. *"Further, this calling would seem to have an attraction for these folks, as the family names today met with upon the boats are among those recorded in connection with canal boat inspection and probably this family continuity with canal boat life goes back much further."*

The censuses between 1851 and 1901 show this to be very much the case, especially for the Ashcroft family who appear prominently in the inspection registers of the 1920s and 1930s. At least two of the boats on the earlier censuses, the *'Ann'* and the *'Kenneth'* were still worked during this period, crewed by descendants of the Ashcroft family. In all the inspections made in this period, the Ashcrofts crewed on almost every working boat . The inspector reported in 1929 that the *'Kenneth'* crewed by Joseph Ashcroft had *"an exceptional clean and tidy cabin".*

Some cabin inspectors were more particular than others, inspecting the brassware or turning the beds over. They had the authority to impound the boat if they were not satisfied. Living conditions on board the Lancaster boats were generally reported as being to the satisfaction of the inspector who went as far as to say *"Respecting cleanliness of cabins, in a few there was room for improvement, yet on the other hand some were very creditable, a pleasure to enter.* He further went on to say that the *"best kept barges in this respect are those having a woman on board."* John Brydone, the first inspector to be appointed under the Canal Boats Act of 1884, reported the opposite view of the boats he had encountered in other areas. *"I found the cleanest kept boats were almost invariably those on which there was no woman but worked entirely by men."*

A Medical Officer of Health's Opinion

On 20 February, 1930 an article appeared in the *'Municipal Engineering, Sanitary Record and Municipal Motor'* journal, entitled *"The Public Health Department" "From the Desk of a MOH"* and said *"On health grounds the life on a canal boat has much to commend it"* and admitted a certain amount of envy of a boatman he had met *"who has charge of a boat, has reached the age of thirty-eight and has never slept in a bed ashore. Born on a canal boat one of seven, all alive and engaged in going down to the canal in boats, he finds it a grand life and envies no one."* He imagines this particular bachelor meeting some handsome lady of a barge – *"and most of them are fine, upstanding bonny women) who will get him and they will raise a family together, who in turn will follow in his footsteps and live happy and carefree lives amid gaily painted water buckets and glistening brass work."*

Arthur Harry Griffin the famous Preston journalist, in an article in the *'Lancashire Daily Post'* which appeared on 4 September 1934 entitled *'Playing a Modern Tune on old waterways'* also conjured up a romanticised view of canal life. He spoke of:- *"huge shaggy coated horses plodding up and down the sixty miles of tow paths, with the lumbering craft swaying along behind the*

(Courtesy of May Sharp)

swinging barges swaying through the sleepy Fylde." He was very surprised at the discovery of a wireless on board *"the rough boats"* and that the canal folk *"despite the gypsy life are not at all the ragged uncouth barbarians one might be led to expect but are essentially people of character and courage, even possessing in some degree those qualities of refinement, more generally associated with men and women in a higher social sphere and a community of philosophers living close to nature"*

On reading such an article the Preston boatmen would hardly agree with what was written about them. To them the thirties were times of hard work and tough competition and would have no time for philosophising about their life.

"The School Board Chap"

Another official the boatmen's families did not always welcome was the School Board Inspector. Children were often separated from their families from the age of five or six and sent to stay with land-based relatives to allow them to attend school regularly, joining their families at weekends and school holidays. He would often appear at the *'starting place'* at Preston wharf before the boats sailed to check if the children had gone to school.

In 1891 nine year old Ann Ashcroft was boarding at Glasson Dock, whilst her parents Charles and Mary Jane were working the *'Albert'* at Forton. At 35 Edward Street, Preston three canal children, John Woodburn, Nancy Pimley and Mary Ashcroft were lodging. By eight years of age many a boat boy had completed his formal education and worked full time on the boats, sometimes being lent out to other families to help out.

Richard Cross, son of Abraham and Rebecca, said that he and many other children spent their time dodging 'the School Board' and didn't really attend school much after the age of twelve. John Tickle admitted that he didn't attend school as much as he should, especially when his parents were short handed but said that he remembered having an attendance card for schools he went to along the canal. In the nineteen thirties John Parkinson mainly attended St Peter's School in Preston but also went to village schools like Bilsborrow situated along the canal corridor. He never remembers being given any 'homework' and said that by attending different schools, would miss out on some subjects and be taught the same things twice in some instances. John admits to being more 'worldly wise' in more practical matters because of his life on the canal but like many others continued his education in later life, in his case when he did his National Service in Malaya.

In 1922 'Uncle Tom Robinson' (father of Mary Jane, wife of Dan Ashcroft) was given the cane for having dirty clogs. His mother Elizabeth Robinson, John's grandmother was so annoyed she went immediately to the school and 'thumped' the schoolmaster, as John put it, "shutting one of his eyes". She ended up in the magistrates' court, having travelled there by bus with her 'supporters' including her sister, Janet Robinson and was bound over to 'keep the peace' and fined ten shillings.

Parliament Looks Into the Matter

In 1923, an article appeared in "The Schoolmaster" found that no evidence was found to support the critics that canal children's health and moral welfare was any more affected than land-based children but education was a different matter. The committee were practically unanimous that canal boat children are "scandalously under educated" and put an estimate of illiteracy as 85 per cent. They recommended that after a period of grace of a year to enable arrangements to be made, children of school age should be prohibited from living on canal boats during school terms. At the beginning of the century ninety per cent of boats had children aboard, but by 1931 there were thirty three boats inspected with no children of school age at all.

May Ashcroft's older sisters had been boarded out during term time, only joining their parents on the canal boats during school holidays. May carried a *'travelling card'* with her which she presented at each school as proof of her regular attendance. One day on being summoned by the headmistress, thinking she was in trouble, was told that she was doing extremely well and was way ahead of the other pupils.

A Changing Situation

In the next twenty years or so most boatmen and their families were living in houses near the Preston canal basin, Edward Street, Nixon's Row, Ladywell Street and Back Canal Street and in 1927 the inspector had put in his annual report that *"most people have houses at Preston, boats showing a decline in the occupancy of the canal boats by women and children, being their homes during trips only."*

When the children got older and able to look after the house, maybe making sure the other kids went off to school their mother would often join her husband on the boat. By the end of the nineteen thirties, the inspectors were making only cursory inspections of the boats as traffic on this canal was coming to a close.

THE BAINES FAMILY - BOAT OWNERS

The writing is on the wall

By 1931 the major carriers were the Baines Brothers, James, John and Lawrence, whose father Thomas and uncle John crewed *'Wasp'* and *'Redwing'* in 1881. When Wigan Coal & Iron Company went out of business in 1928, they sold their vessels to the Baines's. Gradually Baines's bought out other firms such as Hampton's of Preston who had a small fleet of vessels, and the firms of S R Thompson and W I Turner of Lancaster as these firms also ceased trading on the canal..

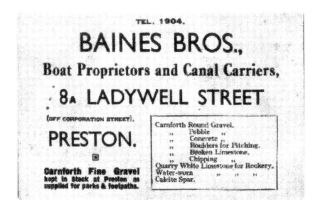

Their premises were in Ladywell Street, a street which ran from Marsh Lane to the coal yards at the end of the canal basin. On one side was a row of small terraced houses, on the other side was the canal basin or turning point, which stretched all the way to Bridge Street at the top of Fylde Road. House numbers 1 – 4 are still there but No. 5 is now a car park. 8a Ladywell Street was a former public house *"The Jolly Tars"* whose entrance was in Mount Pleasant, to run their business, a fitting place for prominent members of the Fylde Road Primitive Methodist Church!

Thomas Baines and his wife Mary ,nee Walmsley

The Baines' carried on trading until 1944 at the time when the wartime coal zoning order was in operation. They had been experiencing trouble with the boatmen, who by this time were members of the *'Transport and General Workers Union'* and were making demands regarding wages and conditions. Rather than being forced into agreements with their workers, and with the traffic to Kendal gas works dwindling, the Baines Brothers decided to sell the business to the bargees, selling them for about £30 each.

Six of the Best

Six of the boats were sold to the Ashcroft family. to whom they were related by marriage. These were *'No. 15 Ann'*, *'No. 16. Wasp'*, *No. 32 'Harold'*, *No. 34 'Herbert' No. 41 Kenneth and No. 48 Benjamin.* In 1942 Daniel Ashcroft senior formed *'Ashcroft Canal Carriers Limited'* along with his three sons who continued to take coal to canal-side mills in Lancaster until the mill switched to oil in 1947 and they surrendered their boat registrations.

A Long Pedigree

The Baines family had had been connected to the canal in some way to the beginning of the nineteenth century. John Baines born in 1800, went on to become captain of one of the packet boats. His brother, William reported as being drunk at the time, was drowned in Glasson Dock in 1849, eleven years after the body of his two year old son Lawrence was found at the lock gates, after playing by the canal.

John's brother Lawrence, born in 1802, had two sons Thomas and John who were both boatmen. Thomas was christened in 1847 at Holy Trinity, Preston. He appears on the 1861 census as mate of an unnamed boat at Forton, near Lancaster, with his elder brother John as master. In both the 1871 and 1881 censuses he is master of *'Wasp'* with his wife Mary and children. Thomas's three sons, Lawrence, James and John were later to form Baines Brothers.

Thomas' wife was Mary, nee Walmsley. The uncle of Mary was Thomas Walmsley who was president of the Preston Temperance Society after the death of Joseph Livesey, the founder of the movement. Thomas' widow Alice was connected with various temperance organisations in the town She was a Congregationalist, took great interest in the local lodge of *'Good Templars'* and donated one hundred pounds towards the new Temperance Hall.

Thomas and John also had a sister called Margaret (1843 – 1866) who was married to Joseph Hampton, boatman. Margaret died very young, possibly giving birth to her daughter Jane. Joseph married Ann from the Ashcroft boating family three years later. Jane also was to go on to the canal with her husband Joshua Robinson and *'foster child'* John Tickle who later worked for a time on the canals with a cousin of Jane's, Jack Baines'.

The name *'Lawrence'* appears in every generation of the Baines family and the censuses of 1881, and 1901 show a Lawrence Henry Baines born in 1844 at Glasson Dock as a canal carter in Dukinfield, Cheshire. In 1891 he is a *'blacksmiths' striker'*. It is probable that he was also a son of Lawrence and Elizabeth.

"Any supplies for t'boat?"

Lawrence, one of the three brothers who later were to form 'Baines Brothers' was born in 1868 in Holme, Westmorland. In his early twenties he was with his wife Mary on an unnamed boat at Priest Hutton. In 1913 he is listed as a grocer at 57 Marsh Lane, at the corner of Ladywell Street. Next to the shop was the *'Boatman's Arms'* with a stable yard. The directory for 1922 shows Lawrence as a boat owner at the same address, with his wife Mary still running the grocer's shop.

Lawrence Baines and family

The Baines family were renowned for their good works and during the First World War Mary used to entertain the wounded soldiers from Mount Street Hospital in the parlour at 57 Marsh Lane, together with her daughters Elizabeth and Janie. Alice Hurst, grand-daughter of Lawrence remembers as a very small child peeping round the curtains to watch the soldiers as they sat taking tea and listening to the piano. The ladies of the family were often unofficial midwives and baked cakes for the canal families.

James Baines born in 1884 was one of the youngest of Thomas and Mary's family. He too was to help run the boats from Ladywell Street and with his wife Bertha (nee Cross) had two daughters, May and Janie. Janie was born in 1905 on a canal boat.

The family moved on to *'dry land'* at 8 Ladywell Street around 1908 and it was from here that James managed his boats for several years, using a room in the house as his 'office'. Dorothy Green, his grand-daughter owns a small chest of drawers that came out of one of the boats and has vivid childhood memories of visiting.

From 1910 to 1926 James was a member of the Preston Borough Police force and in 1922 was living at 8 Nixon's Row, a continuation of Ladywell Street. He was still involved in the day to day running of the business. Another brother was John *'Jack'* Baines born 1872, who on the 1891 census was with his wife Ellen on 'Kate'.

These people on *'May, No. 35'* taken around 1910 have been identified by descendants as Jack, his daughter Elizabeth by his first wife Ellen, Janie his second wife and their baby Tom Baines.

The name of Baines, was therefore connected to the Lancaster Canal for almost a hundred and fifty years. They all originated from north of the county and for the most part settled in the Preston area. Some branches of the family, such as William Baines, whose father and brother had tragically drowned at Glasson Dock moved to Bradford where his descendants live to this day. He emigrated to Utah in 1885 having converted to Mormonism after his marriage and has been *'credited'* with several different wives. Rumour abounded in the family about a Baines being hung for sheep stealing, having resorted to this crime to feed his family but this has never been proved.

A list of Baines' boats, most of which appear in the *'Journal of Canal Inspections 1929 – 1938'*, held in the Lancashire Record Office.

Ann No. 15
Benjamin No. 48
Clara No. 49
Express No. 7
Farewell No. 47
Harold No. 32
Herbert No. 44
Iron Duke No. 9
Joseph

Kenneth No. 41
May No. 35
Nellie No. 53
Prince of Wales No. 3
Redwing No. 17
Sarah No. 38
Venture No. 26
Wasp No. 16

'Joseph' at Garstang

MEMORIES OF JOHN TICKLE (1905 – 1988) AND A LAUGH WITH A SALWICK CHARACTER

John Tickle was born in 1905 in Preston. His mother died five days after giving birth, at the age of twenty three and his father, unable to bring him up on his own asked Joshua Robinson and his wife Jane, who had no children, to look after him. He offered to pay them 6/8d a week until such time as John was old enough to earn his own living. They were willing to do this to provide the boy with a loving home and he was treated like their own son, for a time going under their name. John's great grandparents were Daniel Ashcroft and Elizabeth Beesley whose other granddaughter Elizabeth Tickle was a visitor on board *'Kenneth'* at Lound Wharf in 1881.

Joshua was formerly a coal merchant and Jane had handled boats from childhood with her parents Joseph Hampton and Ann Ashcroft, her stepmother. Her mother Margaret, Joseph's first wife, was the daughter of Lawrence Baines and sister of John and Thomas Baines

Listening to John, it becomes very clear that the boatmen on this particular canal possessed many fine qualities. They were honest, hardworking and helpful to one another, extremely resilient and a generally happy breed, even in times of adversity. His reminisces cover mostly the period of his childhood to the mid-nineteen twenties when he left the canal and took steady jobs, first at Preston Docks, and later working for Chris Miller's of Preston, a company famed for heavy road haulage and their large mobile cranes. Although *'Jos'* and Jane were not his real parents, John constantly refers to them as *'mum and dad'* and after Jos died suddenly on the canal in 1918 when John was thirteen, he carried on working with

Jane until she reached her sixties and retired.

From the horse's mouth
He describes the scene at Preston Wharf on a typical Sunday morning in great detail. *"It starts when the boatman and his wife get up, not too early, about seven o clock. Some of the boats have already come in on the Saturday but there are still some to arrive on Sunday morning. The lady would make the breakfast and tidy the cabin while the captain went off to the stables with proven for the horse. After breakfast the captain would return to the stable to make sure the horse has eaten up, been watered, given some hay, then the stable would be cleaned out, not forgetting the harness, which they called "gears". By this time the children would have gone off to church. The Catholics off to St. Walburge's, the Church of England off to St Mark's, St Peter's and St George's. After lunch the children then go off to Sunday school whilst the captain and his mate or wife make final preparations and tidy the boat.*

Very particular are the boat people about the horse's collar, cos' if that's wrong, everything's wrong. The horse is their living. So the horse can't wear a town horse collar, got to be an open top collar shoved on through its neck, not over its head, and its got to be padded from about two and a half to three inches from the top and two and a half to three inches off the bottom, padded so its not touching the horse when it's hauling the boat. The lining is usually of flock, relined and recovered, covered by shirting, what's been washed and washed and will not harm the horse.

On Sunday teatime, the captain goes up on the coal side to choose his load. Wigan Coal have a private tip of their own. The captains choose their load in their turns, there's loads for Garstang Gas, Carnforth Gas, Kendal and Wigan and Iron coalyards and individual wharves up and down the canal.

Sunday night is the night when most of the captains of the boats go for a drink. They all have their favourite pubs in Preston; 'Fleetwood Arms', 'Beehive', 'Barley Mow', 'Boatman's Arms', 'Fylde Tavern,' 'Ship Inn' in Fylde Road and the 'Sun' in Friargate.

The talk's all boating; they know nothing else, its all talk about the boat, the horses, his mate, his wife, his kids.

First thing Monday morning the boats are all ready to be turned round in Leighton Street basin, the starting place. All the boats are turned round, shoved up in the muck fields, stern first, off up to the coalyard. First boat under the tip loads forty eight to fifty tons of coal tipped in stern end first, middle end next, bow end next. The good captain, he can load that boat as easy as water in a saucer.

By now the shops have started to open they opened earlier them days and the captain's wife goes to order the proven for the horse at Joe Needham's in Marsh Lane, or Bretherton's in Corporation Street, goes down to get her groceries and tells Joe Needham what time the boat will be down in the muck fields.

The mix for the proven for a decent size horse or pony to last an ordinary Lancaster trip is two score of crushed oats, two score of bran and two bags of chopped hay which is approximately three days feed for the horses to Lancaster and back.

When the wife returns with the groceries, they shove the boat out and pick up the proven out of the muck field. The canal office official then comes out to read the lead plates on the boat bow and stern, makes a note of the tonnage, goes back into the office to make out a ticket which the boatman collects and puts in the cabin.

The captain would then go across to the stables, put on the gears and away they would go on their journey northwards.

It was usual to walk with the horses to Stocks bridge as the cutting from Maudland bridge to Fylde Road bridge had coping stones all along, so it was safer to walk with them through there, then walk round Steam Mill, go over the wooden bridge at Low Basin bottom at the end of Tulketh Brow, getting on at the next bridge.

John Tickle and horse

The boat would then be washed down, even though it had only gone a short distance and it would be time for cups of tea, a bit of lunch and on to "Four Mileston" where the stables are. The first stables out of Preston used to be at Lea Road bridge, two three-stall stables and a bank house near the wooden top bridge.

At Woodtop bridge, they would get off with proven for the horses, putting the buckets on which were specially made by Talbot's of Fylde Street. ruffling up the proven which was always damp so that it wouldn't blow away in the wind. While the horses were having their feed, the captain would do odd jobs on the boat such as preparing the lamp in case they would be travelling in the dark.

Next stop would be just before Hollowforth bridge. They would jump off the boat, not as easy as it sounded as the land would be a fair distance from the boat, so they would pull in by using a 'shaft' or bargepole, made out of pitch pine with a hook on the bottom. They would get to the bank, the shaft thrown or handed to his wife and bucket on the horse again.

'Hand and Dagger' bridge, near Salwick Wharf is now approaching. The captain may call out "Do you want some cheese from t'Dagger'?" "Aye, better get some cheese." He then walks with the horse through a gatehole and on to the bridge.

When the horse was seen through the bridge, he would go back up the steps back through the road to the Hand and Dagger pub, get a pound of cheese and a pint of beer. By this time the boat has passed and he catches up to the boat at the next bridge. The horses are now right until Swillbrook, a distance of eight miles, where he gets off at Stone Chimney bridge, gets out a bucket of proven for the horse, some for the pony, buckets on and away they go again.

Next stop the 'Roebuck', buckets on again, the third meal in twelve miles. "Do you want owt from Post Office?" "Aye, we want some bread." The captain's wife would go on the tiller and the captain would go to the post office for two loaves of home baked bread."

Another gill or pint at the White Bull, catch the boat at the next bridge. It is probably now about six or seven o'clock at night so a decision has to be made as to where to stop for the night. A favourite stop is Stubbins, fifteen miles from Lancaster ready for an early start next morning to be in Lancaster by dinnertime. Sometimes they went another four miles to Ford Green to give themselves a better start.

As it goes dark, the lamps are lit. The steering lamps consisted of a metal case with glass at the side and front. The lamp was only small and couldn't be too bright, as it might dazzle the horse who could manage quite well in the dark as the lamp would light all the stonework on the bridges. All the bridges on the Lancaster canal had a whitewashed archway, When a boat passed under the bridge, there wasn't much room without touching the sides. If the boat was bumped too much there was danger of leaking.

At last they reach Ford Green, its getting late but still the horse has to be brushed own, dried and fed. He is led to the stable down a path but the doors are shut, not a good sign, usually meant someone was in. "Aye, aye anybody in?" The stables especially in quiet places were often used as shelter for the night by passing tramps. If there was no answer, the boatman would strike a match, he always had a bit of candle in his pocket, and has a look around. Tramps would never be turned out, but once he was there he would be in for the night. After the horse had been tended to, the door would be fastened with a stick, and there the tramp would have to stop till the next morning, in case he were a wrong' un.

Up next morning bright and early about five o'clock, the collar for the horse would have been warming by the fire, the captain would go to the stable and then untie the boat. The boat was then shoved off the side, horses out with buckets on and they're away. The captain's wife would make the breakfast which would be taken on deck by the captain, maybe a pint of tea and toast. The same procedure is followed with the horses to make sure they were fed and watered. The boat horses got so used to canal water after a week or two that they wouldn't touch tap water. The bucket had to be clean though or they'll wet you with it.

The next stable was at the other side of Cockerham at a place called Gillows Hall, known to the boat people as 'Gillers'. (This hall is now better known as Leighton Hall, once home to the famous Gillow furniture family.) Proven time again then away towards Bay Horse and Ellel Grange where the scenery is at its best Relax until you come to Lodge Hill. There you would have to get off with the horse and take it through the bridge until it landed at the branch off Glasson Dock. This was all for the safety of the horse.

Now over the bridge away through Galgate eventually landing just under three miles off the first high bridge at Lancaster called Three Milestone High Bridge through a lovely avenue of trees.

On arrival at Lancaster there were lots of other boats more or less for the different mills, 'White Cross', 'Electric Works', 'Bath Mill' and the coalyards, 'Wigan Coal' and 'Turners'. At Lancaster men were looking for work discharging the boats walked down the bank to meet the boats for jobs. Not all were dischargers, some were mates of boats. Some boats picked up men along the way who were willing to work. The men would ask the captain to lend him a shilling and that would make sure that you would hire him and guaranteed that job and if they let you down there was no more, one told the other and they would lose their living.

The time spent discharging would depend on how many men were available to help. It usually took two men to discharge a boat loaded with fifty tons. They would have two barrows going which would hold anything up to four hundredweight of coal - if you're barrowing it off on a wharf at the mills you start with one barrow on the bow deck. The barrow is on two planks to keep the barrow right, one plank won't do, as the barrow has two legs." If there's three of you, one would be the wheeler, he wheels both barrows but when he brings one barrow back and drops it and one barrow isn't full, he doesn't stand with his hands in his pockets, he gets going on the top to help out."

There were some characters amongst the dischargers. Two of the better known ones were 'Country Dick', a very old frail man but a 'real good workman'. No-one knew anything about him or where he came from.

The best known was 'Irish Johnny' who was as John put it "the dirtiest man that ever came out of Ireland. If he got a fresh shirt, he put it over the top of one that was already there and he if got another jacket it had to be another size bigger, an overcoat on top of that and same with his trousers. He never cast a thing. He used to carry a pack with his belongings in and was that filthy of a man. He called the English people and talked to himself and when he finished with you discharging you were glad to get rid. Nobody could ever get to know what was in his pack but nobody could lift it He went missing one time for weeks and weeks, and nobody knew where he had disappeared to. He had gone for short periods before, maybe muck spreading for a farmer but always turned up. People started to get concerned about him.

Then somebody saw him in Garstang, he had been in the workhouse. To their surprise he wasn't an old man at all but young. Before, he had a beard, a great dirty beard he had, pack on him and he must have weighed about twenty stone with all the packing he had. He didn't return to the canal until he went back into his old uniform. Sadly one day he was found at Carnforth, he had died at the roadside and that was the end of Irish Johnny.

The mills at Lancaster were just past Penny Street Bridge to the right, down the footpath, the coal yards on the opposite side of the canal. Whilst the men were unloading, his wife, son or daughter would go back to the stables with the horse, about a quarter of a mile away. Rent for the stables would be about two shillings a month and for this amount you could get a three-stall stable . The boatmen who had only one horse or a horse and *pony could share the rest of the stable and would only have to pay a shilling a month.*

The horses were then fed and checked to see if they needed to go to the blacksmith for shoeing and then they were led back to the stables. The ladies would then perhaps go shopping or may even help with the discharging if the men were short handed.

When all this was finished and the boats emptied, they were turned round at the basin. The time would probably be three or four o'clock. Geared up and away they went again. The boat people might have a good wash in the canal water or if they were lucky they could have a wash at the mills. The next job is for the boats to be washed off. It didn't matter that they were going to get loaded again tomorrow, the dust still had to be cleaned off. Very particular the boat people are about keeping the boat clean. A decision would have to be made about how far they would go before turning in for the night. It was usually 'Gillers', eight miles out of Lancaster leaving twenty two for the next day. Or maybe a little further making it easier to get loaded to get back to Preston for mid afternoon the following day.

Back to Preston again, ready for the next day when the routine would start all over again, loading the boats for the different companies.

On a weekday, the canal children would go to school at nine o'clock, the main ones in Preston were St Walburge's, All Saints, and St Peter's. They knew that their family's boat would have left about ten o clock and by the time school was finished would be well on their way. A gang of them, maybe three of the Ashcrofts, some of the Robinsons would go to the railway station catch the train and get off at Broughton or Barton stations and walk to Hollowforth bridge, a distance of ten miles on the canal, only about five by rail. They would look to see if their boat had come through yet, their family would leave a marker such as a pile of slack on the bank. They knew the tell-tale signs, no horses' footmarks would tell them to start walking back towards Preston and have a good look from the bridge.

They would see the boat perhaps half a mile away by the smoke. Sometimes the boat had already passed an hour or more before. Some of the children may have got off the train further along at Brock, Garstang or Catterall but it would be doubtful that the boat had got that far, Getting off a Brock Station, would be a good distance, if the boats were half an hour in front or behind them, they would be able to see it. The kids had their landmarks, they knew the country lanes, ways across the fields, through farmyards where they would often be offered a cup of milk and piece of pie. At holiday times the children would help with the boat and with the horses.

This gradually came to an end, children tramping up and down when families started having houses in Preston. The lady then would maybe go off the canal to the house until one or two of these kids got bigger and capable of looking after the house and making sure the other kids went to school."

Some of the trips were further north than Lancaster but John's family did not do many of those. 'Wigan Coal and Iron's' boats mostly went to 'Kendal Coal and Gas', a distance of fifty seven miles and the money would be very good, approximately double the Lancaster trip money, because of the seven locks at Tewitfield.

This slowed the journey down, and would be hard work. If there were only two people to a boat, one had to be the steerer and the other had to set off on his bike to work the locks. At Chapel Bridge, half a mile before the bottom lock, he would put the bucket on the horse and set off on his bike to the lock. *"All the time the horse on his mind, as there is a stable approaching, will the horses pass them or go in? He's winding the paddles, letting water out, going up to the top gates, winding them, closing paddles and running over the bridge to check on the horse.*

By the time the boat has landed, the locks are dropped, the horse pulling up Lock Hill. The boatman stops there, hooks off three coils in his hand, catches it round the bridge which is only narrow, pulling the boat in the lock, the boat enters the lock, and the man is at the top gate. As soon as it touches the counter arch he leaves the horse, gets hold of the line to hold the boat in and then runs back right to the bank side to shut the gate. His mate or wife is now climbing up the other lock gate, no steps then like there is now, there's a ladder now, you used to have to climb up every lock gate.

79

You're shoving that gate to and you'll both have a bit of a pant and it's filling up.

He then goes to the next lock and repeats the same operation until they get to the top. Now everything gets easier and at times like this with the lovely countryside around them they think what a great job this is, now we're finished with the locks till tomorrow.

Wind and rain were the most regular hold-ups, especially around the Cockerham and Glasson Dock area with the wind coming in from the sea. There were times when it was difficult to get off the boat with the wind pinning it down, the boat going on the side and getting stuck in the reeds and mud.   The horses would then be taken to the nearest stable to be fed rather than struggle on the bank; but a start would be made whatever the weather."

After a short spell working for the Hamptons, Jos and Jane went to work for Thompsons of Lancaster, running the 'Stella', a very strong boat but hard to pull. From there to the 'Florence', a lighter boat. The opportunity to crew different boats came when a boatman got a job in town or went to work for other companies such as 'Baines Brothers' or 'Wigan Coal and Iron.'

The next boat they moved up to was the 'Wasp', "a lovely boat" and also the 'Kenneth' which Jane was very proud of, "just right for all her ornaments". She had special furniture made and John said all the inspectors gave her credit for her cabin.

Seed's Directory of 1904

Entry in Barrett's Commercial Directory 1960. Turners were still trading after the canal ceased commercial carrying of coal.

81

Fourteen and prepared for manhood

In October 1918 John had officially left school. During the war he had from time to time not attended and had helped his parents when no other help was available. He got employment away from the canal, but it didn't last. The job was an errand boy at Heaney's of Chapel Street and John remembers once taking a delivery of two or three dishes of jugged hare to a big house at the top of Penwortham Hill, on his bicycle. Struggling to take the big heavy bike up the hill he fell dropping the groceries in the road. He gathered them up as best he could, left them on the step, knocked on the door and got back quickly on his bike downhill back to Preston. By the time he got back to the shop he was sacked. That suited John, he was back on the canal once more. While he had been absent, his parents had hired a man called Jack Isherwood to steer for them. He was quite old and the job was getting too much for him, out in all weathers. A day or two after John came back to work he said *"Well, you've got t'lad back, Jos, I think I'll turn in."* What he meant was he would turn in to the workhouse, then the only option for those without means of support and a home.

Life carried on; his mother in the first boat, Jos following behind in the second one that was being towed, which was referred to as the *'extra boat'* and John looking after the horses. John reflects that he should have steered for Jos in the winter, letting him go down in the cabin, but his father would have none of it. *"He would be dressed in a coat, an old trilby hat with a piece of string tied round so it wouldn't blow away and he would be singing away all day, wet, hail, rain, as happy as a lark and my job came to be quite easy".*

In 1917 Jos and Jane Robinson, and John were running the *'Kenneth'* and the *'Wasp,'*. One day Jane was collecting her trip money from Thompson's Office in Lancaster and was told of their plans to use a *'steamer'* off the Leeds – Liverpool canal to replace the horses. This was a blow as it would mean less money; the steamer could only carry loads of 36 tons. Jos was needed to act as mate on the steamer leaving Jane and John to run their boats alone.

Tragedy hits a family

The steamer only lasted about six months, they went back to horses, but by Easter the following year, tragedy struck. On Good Friday Jos was at the tiller of *'Wasp'* following behind other boats, Jane being on *'Kenneth*, sailing from Lancaster to Garstang when he was suddenly taken ill. When they arrived in Garstang, Tom Baines told one of his crew to take over the steering for him while Jane made her husband comfortable in the cabin. John took over *'Wasp'* and on arrival in Preston was sent to fetch the *'shilling doctor'* from his surgery in Fishergate Brow. Sadly, Jos died on Easter Monday 1918 aged fifty five. After the funeral, Tom Baines said to Jane *"There's only the two of you now, you can't manage two boats between you. I'll take 'Wasp' and you and the lad can have the 'Kenneth'."* Jane agreed as Tom had a large family to support.

Manhood has arrived

John was now the man of the family and they carried on but Jane worried about John having all the responsibility. Help was always on hand with boatmen like Dan Ashcroft to give advice and to find suitable horses, and John remembers Dan's brother Charlie, *"a real gentleman"* who ran the *'Sarah'* and *'Ann'* for Turner Brothers in Fleet Street, leaving to get a job in town horse driving and offering Jane a *'gallower'* (this is a *'Galloway'* – a type of horse known for its capacity for work, a small horse of about fourteen hands which could walk under most bridges.) for ten pounds, complete with *'gears'*.

John always said that his mother should have been a sergeant major, not a boatwoman. Everything had to be right. He said *"It were nowt to break ice down t' side o' t'boat for a bucket of water to get washed with first thing in morning, no pampering, boil some water and get washed. It would be a crime for any boatman to go in Lancaster on a Sunday afternoon mucked up. He'd never be forgiven by any other boatman. Got to be washed and tidied up, the lady steering the boat in Lancaster, clean pinny on and in summertime she'd have one of these fish ladies hats on, that was for the midges. It did two jobs that, kept sun off their head and keep midges out of the way. Your horses would be clean, your gears clean. Lancaster canal from Penny Street Bridge down to as far as Bells bridge which was known as the Lily Wood, on a real length of park, there were more people on that length than were on Ashton Park at Lancaster and that's where a lot of the photographs on the postcards were taken."*

John said that it took two of them about six and a half to seven hours to shift the coal and sometimes as much as eight or nine hours. John was only fourteen but had to try to keep up with the rest of the boatmen discharging. His mother told him if he couldn't, *"You mun pay 'em a shilling a piece out of eight shillings we get at White Cross for helping out."* After the work was finally done, John often joined the other boatmen in the evening going down to the *'Hippodrome'* (theatre/music hall) in Lancaster finishing off with fish and chips at Penny Street, bringing some home for his mother.

Eventually Jane decided to retire, much to the disappointment of John. After she left he tried to get work on the docks. One afternoon he was asked to help Abe Cross at Ratcliffe Wharf at Forton, along with a chap called Tommy Hanlon. On his bike he went, while Tommy had to walk it, as buses were very few in those days.

They worked solidly until about seven or eight o'clock when Tommy said to him *"Leave thi bike here, Abe'll fetch it back tomorrow and walk it back with me."* They stopped for a drink in Garstang - the first pint of beer that John ever tasted and then they set off walking the fifteen miles walk, all after hauling fifty tons of coal.

Without a regular job, John grew very despondent and made a final attempt to persuade Jane to return to the canal. Her mind made up she turned him down.

Back to the good life

John then teamed up with Jack Baines, working for his father, Tom. John was seventeen and Jack a year older. They were paid by Jack and were not paid any trip money but drew *'discharging money'* from the mills. Jack's mother used to order their groceries at Tom

Shutt's in Marsh Lane and proven was bought from either Joe Needham's, Bretherton's in Corporation Street or Pye's at Lancaster.

One trip they were coming out of Lancaster, the horse marching on. It was a good horse, they thought it had been a *'tram horse'* in Morecambe. It was a good all-rounder, going by itself in the dark but used to walk right at the edge through the bridge holes. The two lads got on well together and got up to all sorts of escapades. One day they had unloaded at Lancaster, discharged,and finished by about five o'clock. They pulled the horse back to the stables ready for morning. *"We're not setting off tonight."* says Jack. *"I think we'll go to the Hippodrome on Dalton Square."* John recalls *"I don't even know if we'd even been washed, but probably, you had to be fairly presentable and we came out of the Hippodrome then decided to go to the pictures, second house. After that fish and chips in Penny Street."*

On the way back Jack said he thought they ought to set off that night and told John to make a bit of proven up while he geared up the horse. Away they went, the horse *"clatter, clatter, clatter"* through the bridges. They made a cup of tea and a sandwich, regardless of just having had fish and chips. They took turns at steering and looking after the horse, one or the other having a sleep in front of the fire in the cabin. They travelled through the night and landed into Preston the next morning, having sailed for ten hours. Tom Baines was waiting on the wharf and asked the lads how far they had come. Jack told him they had set off from *"Stubbins"* that morning but his dad had an inkling that they had travelled from Lancaster through the night.

Tom had a cargo waiting on the tip to be delivered to Ratcliffe Wharf near Cockerham so he told his son to load the boat and set off immediately but insisted on using his own horses as Jack's mare had done enough. He arranged to meet him later at the Roebuck, at Bilsborrow ready to set off that night. Jack wasn't very pleased but his dad insisted, and they took the fifty ton load to Ratcliffe with the fresh horses. Gradually things got back to normal, Tom took his team back and the lads had their horse once more.

John left the canal again later on, getting odd jobs until he finally went to work for Chris Miller. After he got married he felt the lure of the canal again and he asked his new wife if she would like to go on the canal. She said *"it'd be better than a factory"*. He decided against it and never did go back.

Memories from Salwick Wharf – John Holmes

After leaving the suburbs of Preston the canal goes westwards through open country and reaches Salwick, a popular mooring spot. The canal then turns north through a cutting past a canal-side public house commonly known as the Hand and Dagger at Bridge 26. It's true name is the *'Clifton Arms'* and its nickname probably came from the dagger on the Clifton family crest which appears on the sign.

Close to the canal at Salwick wharf are a pair of houses, called *'Station Cottages '*in which a spry old gentleman called John Holmes lived for over eighty years. He never worked on the *'cut,'* but his knowledge of boats and engines were legendary. As a boy he used to play along the canal and got to know the families on the barges as they passed through, with their heavy cargoes. *"They were seventy footers, those barges, they carried loads of up to 45 tons of coal. They worked solidly through the night with only a shovel and a barrow to unload their cargo and by sunrise they were well on their way."* He made friends with the bargees and was sad when he awoke the following day to find they were gone.

"They used to sail through the night in those days, with only an oil lamp in front to guide them, the women used to steer the boats, whilst the men tended the horses." He recalled the harsh winters when there could be fifteen inches of ice on the canal, which the bargees had to smash with their barge poles.

 John recalled the lighter side of life on the canals. Years ago his *'local'* was the nearby *'Hand and Dagger'* and he remembered one particular night a local lad annoying one of the boatmen in the bar. The boatman, who like most of them was a solidly built man, lifted the lad up by the scruff of the neck, and marched him out of the pub, along the canal bank and straight into the moonlit waters of the canal.

John remembered the pleasure cruising in the summer on the converted coal boats, the passengers in their Sunday best were a marvellous sight to see. On their return journey to Preston at night, he recalled how raucous both the men and women could be after they had had a few drinks at hostelries along the way.

Qualified without training
On listening to John one got the impression that he did not altogether agree with the trend for pleasure boating today and talked disparagingly of the skills of the modern boater. Dan Ashcroft also shared this opinion and to him it was incredible that to drive a car meant passing a test but to steer a boat on the canal required no such assessment of competency. Nowadays the new breed of boaters are offered *'helmsman courses'* to better their skills and have confidence on negotiating the waters, which would probably be considered a waste of time and money by the old canal boatmen who learned their skills from their fathers and grandfathers.

John died in 2004 at about eighty four years of age. He lived life very simply but exactly how he wanted, resented interference from doctors and anyone in authority and was resolute in his determination to spend his days along the canal he loved. He had his way in the end.

On the canal at Bolton-le-Sands – 'Clara' owned by J Hampton

The horses are feeding whilst working at the Carnforth bridge, (128,) about 1905.
John Parkinson believes the boat to be the *'James'* and the young boy James
Robinson, his uncle. On the boat is John's great granddad Thomas Robinson who
lived in the first house on the right of the picture.

THE TRUSTY CANAL HORSE

Boatmen generally regarded their horses as an investment to care for. Fodder was stored in the bows of the boat and every few miles along the canal bank there were stables where the horses could rest overnight. (Here we see Thomas Ashcroft with a means by which he earned a living.)

Equine accommodation

Many of the stables had originated from the days of the swift packet boats. No trace of such buildings exist at either the Kendal or Preston ends of the canal but a few along the route survive such as the 'Jolly Roger' at Catforth, at Farleton, Carnforth, and Clifton Hill Bridge, The main stable buildings are now the premises of the 'Waterwitch' public house, on the wharf near Penny Street bridge in Lancaster, rebuilt in the 1980s after a fire in the original buildings. This block consisted of six stables with three stalls with a midden at each end and it was up to the boatman stabling the horses to keep it clean.

Going north to the canal company yard at 'Change Bridge' were three stables, one of which was run by Tom Newby, a canal boatman who used to run the 'Kenneth' before the Robinsons. They were always known as "Tom's stables" and when he retired, no-one took them over.

There were odd stables dotted out along the canal side that were unsupervised, with no ranger's cottage and these were the places where tramps used to go in for shelter. When a boatman entered he would strike a match and shout out "I'm fastening the door, are you sure you're stopping?" "Aye, I'm stopping", would be the reply. With that the horse would be fed, watered and brushed down, the tramp being left there for the night in peace.

Mary Ashcroft said that boat people were known for their kind treatment they gave to their horses and most of them were bought from dealers at Lancaster. She recalls *"Dan's dad would buy a horse, look after it and fatten it up. Then someone would come on a bridge and say how good it looked." "Does tha want to buy it?"* A deal was done after the buyer's *"Aye".* Then Dan's mother Alice would get angry at the delay and start dancing with rage, going mad on deck *"with sparks coming from her clogs."* Dan's dad would quietly tie up the boat, get his bike off and go to buy another horse.

The bottom fell out of her world

Dan Ashcroft senior was a well known *'character'* who was always willing to lend a hand with the handling of horses. He was a tower of strength to his cousin Jane Hampton when she ran her boat with a young John Tickle after her husband Jos died. On one occasion Jane and John's horse went lame, and Dan came down the bank on his bike to put the horse on the boat for them, which was an easy job for him, *"He were a big strong fella"* says John.

Their little black pony had done enough for the day so their cargo was put in Dan's son *('Joe's')* boat. The next morning they set off with Joe's boat behind them and on approaching Dimples Bridge, near Garstang, Jane said *"You'd better come out, there's something wrong with yon Gallower".* By the time they got to Dimples Bridge at Garstang, the pony was down on the bank, rolling around in pain; he had got the *'gripes'.* (A sharp pain in the bowels). The three of them, John, Jane and Joe Ashcroft set about rubbing it and trying to get it to come round when Joe said *"Do you know, Jane, t'boat's sinking!"* They had been so distracted with the pony that when they had got off they hadn't noticed that the boat had hit a rough stone on the canal bottom and water was coming in on to the cabin floor. The prospect of trying to repair a fifty-ton laden boat did not daunt them in the least. With only the basic tools and equipment the boat was patched up with a mixture of horse manure and tar and with the pony now recovered away they went.

Don't send a lad on a man's errand

Young horses were never used to pull a canal boat; they were usually about eleven or twelve years old before they were suitable for this work. They were referred to as *"second hand'* horses. *"Vanners"* were small ones, under ten or twelve hands, often previously used in cabs or landaus. John says that a townsman would call it a *'pony,'* a boatman would say a *'Gallower'*. This was a Galloway, a Scottish breed famed as pack horses.

If a horse went lame, or was temporarily unable to pull a boat, the boat man or woman had to look for a replacement as soon as possible. A man called *'Tuffy'* Goodier had a field at Lea Brow, where horses could go for rest and recuperation and he also lent out horses, mules or donkeys to the boat people when needed.

The lad makes an ass of the job

The Goodiers were a large family, some of whom were connected to the canal and John Tickle, on Jane's orders was sent on one occasion to look for a horse. Tuffy told him *"Aye, I can lend you summat or I can sell thi summat. I'll tell you what, you can take that mule over there."* Tuffy had two or three left over from the First World War. John landed home with the grey mule and as soon as Jane set eyes on the animal she said *"What the ell's ta getten now?."* Young John said, *"Well it'll do."* And it did all right. It had its strange ways, John had to walk with it and it would pull like mad. *"As soon as it lost hearing of your feet it wouldn't do nowt."* Some horses could walk mostly unsupervised and were referred to as *"backers"*.

One day they set off for Lancaster with the mule but as soon as John got on the boat it stopped walking. John had to get off with it and keep it going, he remembers *"This flaming thing – mother's aggravated with it, we're getting nowt done and we're getting nowhere"*. At the next bridge John put the bucket of proven on the mule, which didn't like anyone or anything touching its ears so you had to be careful with the bucket. It started eating and everything was fine until John took

91

the bucket off and caught its ears. It started backing in the bridge hole and went into the canal. First the hind leg went in, then it tipped over right into the canal, John still hold of the bucket and trying to get hold of the hauling line.

John was hauling and Jane jumped off, both holding the mule till it got tired. Jane said *"Tire the bugger out"* and they hauled him to the side, got hold of its ears, put the hauling line round its neck and Jane shoved it down in the canal. As water squirted out of its ears it quickly jumped up on the bank. As soon as they arrived back at Preston Jane said, *Take that donkey back to Tuffy Goodiers without fail, ger it back!"* Saturday afternoon saw John and his mate Albert Robinson riding the donkey back. This amusing spectacle was seen by a group of prisoners from the nearby jail who waved to them furiously as they made their way along Stanley Street.

The man of the house

John was often sent miles to look for likely horses. Skerton, near Lancaster was well known for the sale of horses and John would go, often without any money, just to look around. He once heard of one on the railway bank at the other side of the River Lune. The trader took him across in a horse and cart down a slipway onto the river bank but the cart and horse started going in opposite directions. John started to get alarmed as he couldn't swim. They managed to reach the other side where he was offered the horse for £12, a high price for a horse that looked worn out. *"He's not reyt, he hasn't enough about him. He can hardly stand up, he's really poor. He's too thin, too lanky."* He returned home empty handed and Jane agreed he'd made the right decision as the horse had probably worked on the tramways at Morecambe and would have been unsuitable.

On looking for horses John, although only young was never afraid to speak his mind. On another occasion he told a trader *"I can't take thissun back, she'll drown me, it'll be out of a home and I'll be out of a home an all. I don't think it has strength to walk to Lancaster, never mind pull a boat tomorrow. I'm not taking it, if he gets down, he'll not get up again. Look at him, all skin and th'hairs off him, he's been on t'floor."*. It was now very late, about eleven o clock at night, he had no transport so John had to set off for Galgate with the money still in his pocket. He ran all the way from Penny Street bridge back to the boat to find his mother lighting the lamp, and as soon as she heard his footsteps *"Where's tha been till now?"* John replied *"I''ve been where tha told me. Got nowt, because it weren't worth bringing, worse than what we have now."*

Jane heard that there was to be a sale of horses left over from the First World War and sent John with fourteen pounds to buy one. They were in a sorry state, either lame or had been gassed and were unfit for canal work. John called them *"broken winded"*. Later walking from Lancaster to Morecambe, he saw a horse attached to a landau, standing idle. John made the driver an offer for the horse but was told it was not for sale. Later that day the horse was still there, so he made another offer which was accepted, and the driver immediately started taking the bridle and reins off. John objected as he needed them to lead the horse back home but the driver insisted that they were not included in the very fair price he was getting for it. John had no choice but to take the belt off his trousers, put it round the horse's neck and lead it that way back to Galgate, probably riding it part of the way.

Boatmen always let each other know when suitable horses came up for sale and Tom Baines told Jane that Albert Cuerden had one at his stables at the *'Boatmans Arms'* in Marsh Lane.

Jane does a man a favour – the deal is done

"Aye, Jane theres a likely sort in fer you, but before we start, I want no 'bantering', the price is reyt, no 'bantering', before you look at him." Ignoring this, Jane asked him how much he was going to take for him. *"He's twenty pounds, no less, there's no need to start 'bantering', I won't accept it."* She said, *"I'll tell thi what, Albert, I'll buy it off you and I'll pay in pound notes but tha has to buy t' lad a pair o' clogs. "* He shook his head but Jane was very insistent *"Tha buys John a pair o' clogs out of that twenty pounds, that's the deal . We're taking it off thi hands as it is"* She got her way eventually and the deal was done.

Sometimes a horse proved unsuitable for the job and this one was no exception. it worked well for a while then started getting temperamental It used to kick out and Jane was not happy with it. She asked the *"expert"* Dan Ashcroft's opinion. *"Is it a wrong un 'Dan?"* He pondered for a while and said *"It doesn't like t' lad, Jane".* Approaching Lancaster they met a man who dabbled in horses on the canal bank, told him they weren't suited with the horse. *"I know a fella that's looking for a horse summat like that, he's a fruit hawker at Scotforth."* A bit of haggling was done and he agreed to buy it for sixteen pounds, a loss of four pounds but Jane was glad to have got rid of the troublesome horse.

Health care for members of the family

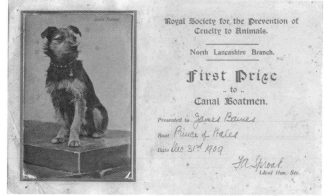

RSPCA Certificate presented to James Baines on *'Prince of Wales'* 1909

A tribute to the Lancaster canal boatmen's treatment of their horses is the RSPCA certificates awarded in 1908 to James Baines of the *'Joseph'* and one the following year for the canal boatmen on the *'Prince of Wales'*.

DROWNINGS IN THE CANAL

There were many reported drownings in the canal. Many canal people never learned to swim and children were particularly vulnerable. The *'Westmorland Gazette'* reported that on 7 September 1907, Ellen *('Nellie')* the four year old daughter of Daniel Ashcroft, boatman of Preston was drowned in the canal at the City o' Pinch wharf where her father, who was master of the *'Iron Duke'* was engaged loading the boat with broken limestone. At the inquest Daniel stated that he had spoken to the child, who was playing about the wharf, only five minutes before he had occasion to go down to move the boat, when he saw her body in the canal. He instantly removed it and called the mother. Artificial respiration was applied to no avail. The jury returned a verdict of *'accidental drowning'* and expressed their sympathy with the parents. Daniel took a photograph of the spot where Ellen had drowned before they left the moorings.

A lunch break for the 'Iron Duke's horse power

An ever present danger Health and safety at work

Reported incidents of drowning were recorded in the *'Canal Workmen's Job Book.'* a document that recorded repairs to the canal, as well as instances of drowning. On 11th May 1901 Alice May Steebles, aged three years eight months of Williams Road, Woodville, Lancaster went out to watch a passing funeral and nothing more was seen of her. She was missing from home from three o'clock and evening search parties were instituted and the canal dragged. Her body was recovered shortly before midnight near to Moor Lane bridge. Last in the company of a child named Jefferson aged four, inference was that the deceased fell into the canal while trying to reach her hat! In those days it was probably not uncommon for a three-year-old child to be left to her own devices.

Many adults were also victims of drowning. The verdict delivered at each inquest hardly differed in each case that was brought before the coroner's court. It was rarely considered accidental; the poor victims were, almost without exception deemed to have been the result of *"suicide by drowning whilst of unsound mind"*. Perhaps the possibility of actually falling into the water was not taken into account.

One unsuccessful suicide attempt was made by a woman called Agnes Hall. In her defence she said that a *'situation'* at Burton that she had applied for had been filled and that she was *'downhearted'* as a result. John Harrison, with the help of Daniel Newby captain of the *'May'* brought her out of the water alive. To add to her distress she was taken before magistrates and sentenced to three months imprisonment for attempting to take her own life by drowning.

In 1910 occurred the drowning of a collector in the employ of a working men's supply company, who according to the inquest *"had for some time been upset in connection with his books and during the last few months had earned only fifteen shillings a week."* He was depressed and a verdict was returned of *"suicide during temporary insanity"*. It seems incredible that no foul play seemed to be suspected even when the victim must have been known to be carrying money.

A farmer, Joseph Park of Deer Park, near Milnthorpe drowned in the canal on 5 February 1901. He had been drinking heavily and at the inquest held, a verdict was returned of *"suicide by drowning whilst temporarily insane."*

As far back as 1823 the following was reported in the *'Lancaster Gazette'*:

Melancholy Accident and Warning.— A respectable farmer, residing near Bank-End, in Cockerham, went to the mill on Tuesday morning, for the purpose of making meal. When this was finished, he unhappily loitered in the village too long, and having entered a public-house there, remained until a late hour. In the morning he was found drowned, having missed the road, which, when sober, he had been accustomed to go along from his earliest days. He has left a large family behind him. What miseries await intemperance!

Canal boatmen were often witnesses to drownings. In 1904 a child of about three years of age was found drowned near the canal workshops, Lancaster by J Baines, captain of the *'Ann'* who immediately pulled him out and applied *'artificial means'* to bring life back to the little boy. There was nothing to indicate how the child had got into the water but he was *"fully dressed with his boots on"*.

In 1904 Samuel Pimley, a boatman found the body of a fifty seven year old woman Elizabeth Worthington, floating in the canal near Stocks Road bridge and on 31 March 1909, it was reported that a body which remained unidentified was found south of Old Hall bridge at 6.15 in the morning by *'boatman Vickers'* of the *'Wegber'*.

One morning John Tickle was sailing to Lancaster approaching Ellel Hall bridge when their horse started behaving very strangely. Jane was at the tiller and noticed that the horse had turned round and was coming back towards the boat. John came out of the cabin, jumped off the boat and tried to turn him round but the horse had no intention of going through the bridge. Eventually he managed to get him through the bridge, put his bucket on and away they went, John walking with him for a while to make sure there was no more trouble. It was only when they landed at Lancaster and started to unload that they were told by another boatman that the local lamplighter had drowned himself at Ellel Hall. Jane now realised why the horse had turned round, even if he hadn't seen the body, he would have smelled it and that explained its behaviour.

One afternoon John Tickle and Jack Baines were returning from Lancaster with an empty boat. As hey approached 'Lodge Hill' at Ellel, Jack got off to guide the horse through the narrow cutting, looked to make sure no other boat was coming, ran over the bank through the bridgehole and saw it was clear. He waited, the horse passed him and away he went through the bridge. The next thing that John saw was Jack dressed up in a frock tailed coat, complete with 'tall shiner' (top hat). He then went out of sight at the back of the bridge, got on the boat and told John not to look round. The coat, tall shiner, umbrella and a note had been found at the back of the bridge and as they got further away, Jack explained that the clothes belonged to an undertaker whose body was in the water. If they had looked round and seen the body, they would have been duty bound to report it and that would have meant a visit to the police station and later the coroner's court to give evidence and precious working time would have been lost.

Bank rangers often found bodies in the water. On 2nd May 1901 the body of Edward Bennett aged 50 was recovered from the canal at Hollinhead Fold basin. Shortly before twelve noon, bank ranger Smith noticed a man peep round a bend in the canal, then disappear. Later he found a coat and hat on the bank. A passing boat brought the body to the surface.

A tale that had been passed down to John Parkinson by his father and grandfather was that they had been sailing along in the moonlight with the lamp on and as they were approaching the bridge at Ford Green they saw a little boy running along the parapet then suddenly disappearing from view. This caused the horses to *"spook"*, breaking the towline and running off. The crew decided to stay in Garstang overnight and on visiting the local public house the landlord told them that earlier that day a little boy had fallen off the bridge into the River Wyre. A strange tale, and as John said *"one that got better with the telling"*.

An unknown boatman with the tools of his trade – a rope and a horse bucket – on the wharf at Lancaster, probably about 1920.

'May' approaching Tewitfield Locks about 1910

Burton wharf in the early years of the century

RECREATION AND PLEASURE TRIPS

The canal has long been popular for recreational purposes. Swimming, fishing, and canoeing are just some of the pastimes that most people can remember from childhood in summer. In winter skating on the canal was popular and a favourite spot in Kendal

was at Highgate Settings. The Kendal Skating Club had bought a field opposite Low Mills called *'Rinkfield'* which could be flooded by opening a sluice gate from the canal to provide, with the help of Jack Frost

Skating at Highgate Settings (Percy Duff collection)

the surface needed. There were other instances of fields being flooded to provide a rink for skaters when the frost came. J H Spencer in the *'Preston Herald'* in 1944 recalled skaters making the journey on moonlit, frosty nights around the waters of Salwick, in the halcyon days of his youth and paints a nostalgic picture of them *"gliding smoothly to and fro in a poetry of motion silhouetted on the gleaming ice, their voices echoing in the sleepy night."*

Fred Lamb, with his sister Dorothy, skating on Glasson Dock basin, 28th January 1933.
(Ruth Roskell collection)

Not all recreational activity was welcomed. On 31st July 1882 young Richard James Rawlinson of Friargate, Preston was found guilty of having thrown a dog with a stone attached to it into the canal. A Public Notice was issued on 1st August as an apology by the boy saying *"I am sorry that I committed such offence, and I promise that I will not in future, do that or any other act to the prejudice of the said Navigation"*. (The words *'navigation'* and *'cut'* were used in the early days as alternatives to *'canal'*.) He went on to say that *"For the leniency shewn to me in this matter by the Police and by the Canal Company, I express my thanks, and undertake to pay for printing fifty copies of this notice."* The usual fine at this time for throwing stones and *other things'* into the canal was a sum up to five pounds. Notices such as these were put up around Preston and Lancaster by the Police and the canal company to deter people from throwing unwanted animals and other debris into the canal and also to *'shame'* the offenders publicly. Getting rid of unwanted of cats and dogs in this way was a common way of disposal at this time. Only later did police stations undertake to dispose of them humanely.

Swimming in the canal was also contrary to the company's bye-laws and another poster reveals two fifteen year old Preston youths caught swimming in the canal, near Shelley Mill publicly confessing their misdemeanour, promising not to bathe in the canal again and to pay any legal expenses incurred. This murky stretch of the canal was warmed by hot water coming from the boilers along underground pipes to cool off in the canal from the nearby cotton factories which drew water supplies from the canal for steam power. David Rigby recalls swimming there in the 1950s and remembers the pipe that led to the canal as being very slimy and dirty.

Charles, son of Annie Lomax (nee Ashcroft) regularly swam in the canal at Ashton in the 1920s and his sister Millie recalls how Charlie would be swimming with a group of friends, their boots and outer clothing on the towpath. A cry would be heard from one of the boys *"Watch out - t' scuffers are coming!"* They would immediately grab their clothes, tie their boots round their neck, and quickly wade or swim to the other side to escape the local bobbies. On one occasion the police were waiting for them but they gave them the slip and were seen running down Fylde Road to Bath Street where one of the boys lived, entered the house and locked the door. Girls were never seen in the canal, it was considered immodest as at that time *'mixed batheing'* at the public baths was not allowed.

Pleasure trips

Another type of passenger travel, the *'pleasure cruise'* on the Lancaster proved to be extremely popular. They may have lacked the comforts of the packet boats of the mid-19th century and by today's standards  were dangerously overloaded but were still a regular event in summer. Often referred to by the boatmen as *'scholar boating'*, the well- scrubbed coal boats were used for Sunday school outings by churches and other organisations. Wigan Coal & Iron used to specialise in such outings and would be approached by a local church to take their entire congregation, sometimes even a piano. Some churches with a large congregation would hire two boats. During the 1922 Preston Guild, Wigan Coal and Iron Company ran passenger boats from Garstang into Preston, giving generous discounts to their customers. The annual Whitsun trip by canal boat from Kendal was thought to be held to take the children away from the evils of the horseracing when Kendal had its own race-course.

In this photograph we see Wigan Coal and Iron Co's boat Wegber being used on a 'scholars' outing at Levens about 1904 (Photo courtesy of the Waterways Trust/ The Boat Museum.

A reyt good do

A Preston newspaper on 27th June 1897 reported on a Jubilee *'treat'* given to *'Preston's Waifs and Strays'* on the occasion of Queen Victoria's Diamond Jubilee.

"The Jubilee treat was given on Saturday afternoon – The children numbering about 950, assembled at the Supper Room, Derby Street, Preston, at one o'clock, and proceeded with banners and flags flying (the girls being headed by the Harris Orphanage Band and the boys of the Trinity Fife and Drum band) through the principal streets to the Canal Wharf, Leighton Street where they embarked on boats, supplied by Mr T Baines, for Mr. Cookson's, Harbour Farm, Salwick. The journey was a most pleasant one. On arrival at about 4.30. coffee, buns and cake were provided. Races were run for prizes, games of football and balloon ascents took place, and a very pleasant afternoon was spent. The return journey was commenced at about 7.45 and on entering the boats each child received a bun or some cake. Preston was reached safely and without accident about 9.30 pm. Mr William Dawson, the honorary manager had full control of all the arrangements, which were carried out most successfully, and he desires to thank all who assisted him in any way whatever."

Zion chapel outing at Sedgwick (Percy Duff collection)

Lawrence Baines, one of the Baines Brothers boat owners, often used his boats to take the Fylde Road Primitive Methodist Church congregation on outings. The boat would be scrubbed out, seating provided and a gramophone provided. He would cut a dashing figure with his trademark bowler hat.

Didn't we have a lovely time

The granddaughter of Charles Ashcroft, Millie Rigby (nee Lomax) remembers the Sunday school trips in the nineteen twenties sailing on a coal barge from Fylde Road, Preston to Ingol, with her parents, brother and sister for the St Mark's Church Annual Field Day. *"It cost 1/6d and we sat on planks of wood which were laid across the boat. We looked forward to it every year."* She talks about the fun they had on the field day with games and refreshments before they set off back on the barge.

Summat new turns up

After commercial trade ceased in the late nineteen forties, Dan Ashcroft, whose family had crewed so many working boats rented a wharf at Cadley from British Waterways from where in summer, he ran pleasure trips from the terminus at Aqueduct Street to the *'Jolly Roger'* at Catforth and back. These trips were very popular for outings and celebrations alike. The *'Jolly Roger'* was a café where the passengers could get refreshments before the return cruise to Preston.

Dan Ashcroft

The first of Dan's boats to take the trippers was an old ship's lifeboat and gradually he acquired and converted more old lifeboats, towing them one behind the other. David Slater of the Lancaster Canal Trust remembers as a boy fishing the canal at Salwick on summer Sundays waiting expectantly for this convoy to come through. Eventually the lifeboats were replaced by a former Leeds and Liverpool short boat, which had originally been horse drawn but now had an engine fitted. Short boats were designed to fit the short wide beam locks of the *'L & L'*, as some of the locks were ten feet shorter than the majority of canals. The *'Shelagh'* had been brought from Leeds onto the Lancaster via Tarleton by Dan with the help of a trawler captain via the River Ribble, River Douglas, the open sea and Glasson Dock. This boat was a prominent feature of the canal, as was its successor, another L & L short boat, *'Leo'* which was renamed *'Shelagh'*.

Change out of ten bob

The *'Shelagh'* is also remembered for the cruises commissioned by the Lancaster Canal Trust during the sixties and seventies, for four full day trips each summer from 1965. Longer cruises were on August Bank Holiday 1968 from Galgate to Tewitfield and return, with a 90 minute stop at Bolton le-Sands and one from Tewitfield to Galgate for which the fare was ten shillings, including the bus which would be laid on to take the trippers back to their starting point. Joe, Dan's brother regularly accompanied these trips and David Slater of the Canal Trust wrote in the 25th edition of their magazine *'Waterwitch'*

Dan and Mary Ashcroft at Galgate

"Round about Cabus, passengers were puzzled by Joe jumping off the boat and disappearing over the bridge whilst the boat carried on. On my first trip I too thought this odd, since nothing was said. However as we approached the junction with the Glasson arm the reason for Joe's departure became apparent. He had walked to the A6, caught the bus to Galgate and so to the locks and had spent the morning going down the flight, setting the locks, then back to the top lock to meet the boat. The trip up and down the flight was always enjoyable, some passengers electing to remain on the boat whilst others took the opportunity to walk."

The trip from Lancaster to Tewitfield would load at Penny Street bridge, and a lunch stop would be made at a pub along the way. For many years the Lancaster Canal Trust also ran campaign cruises to publicise initiatives to protest about the proposal to close the upper reaches of the canal for the construction of the M6 motorway.

The 'Waterwitch' reported how Dan and Mrs Ashcroft had consented to sailing to Tewitfield as 'spearhead' of the rally, which was covered by BBC television. The boat was decorated with bunting and had a poster advertising the rally on the bow. The trips brought pleasure to

'Trying to stop the motorway! LCT Campaign Cruise with John Gavan standing at the back.

thousands of trippers over the years. They came to an end in the mid nineteen seventies because of rising costs. The 'Shelagh' was sold and taken back along the same route via Tarleton that she had

ASSOCIATION FOR THE RESTORATION OF THE
LANCASTER CANAL

Publicity Cruise on the Canal
Sunday, 28th August, 1966
TEWITFIELD to GALGATE BASIN
Depart Tewitfield 9-30 a.m. Prompt
Free bus returns party from Galgate to Tewitfield

Refreshments available   **Price 10/-**

made at the start of her career with Dan once more at the tiller. Sadly she was to suffer the fate of most other boats, being broken up at a Tarleton boat yard.

WALTON SUMMIT BRANCH - THE LOST CANAL

In 1792 an Act of Parliament was passed for a route from Kendal to Westhoughton, consisting of 32 locks and a 600 ft long aqueduct to cross the River Ribble and reach the south end at Walton Summit. This was never achieved mainly because of lack of finance. A branch was built from Bark Hill, New Springs, Wigan called the *'Haigh'* canal to Johnson's Hillock at Wheelton, through the tunnels at Whittle-le-Woods to the Duke of York basin on to Walton Summit. A horse drawn tramway was built in 1803 over the River Ribble, in operation until the 1860s, mainly to bring coal from south Lancashire. It ran from the end of the Lancaster canal near the Corn Exchange on Wharf Street, tunnelled under Fishergate and on to the corner of Ribblesdale Place from where its route can still be seen, through Avenham Park to the top of the steep slope above the *'Old Tram Bridge'*. Tubs of coal were pulled up this slope by a steam-operated winding engine on the site of the present shelter.

Former canal basin at Whittle-le-Woods (Eric Bell)

At the *'Duke of York'* public house in Whittle was a canal basin, called after the pub. Millstones had been quarried out of the hills around Whittle-le-Woods for centuries. After the Lancaster canal was opened and a link made to the Leeds - Liverpool in 1816, they were despatched worldwide from the wharf which had a crane to load the millstones onto the boats, as well as wharves with coal yards, weighing machines and a smithy. To get to the basin, boats coming from Chorley passed along the Lancaster canal and under the tunnels at Whittle. Stone from Whittle Hill quarries, coal and other goods were unloaded onto the adjoining wharf. This section of canal was drained in 1969 and *'Duke Basin'* filled and grassed over when it had fallen into disuse.

In 1985 a monument consisting of four mill stones, one of which was salvaged from the canal bed, was set up to commemorate the past history of this site. Whittle Hills Tunnels were originally one single tunnel, 259 yards long. After a collapse it ended up as two short tunnels with a 150 yard cutting between them. Aqueduct Bridge was built in 1760 to carry the Lancaster canal over the River Lostock leading to the tunnels at Whittle, which had fallen into decay but which have been recently cleared by volunteers.

From the *'Top Lock'* at Johnson's Hillock the old canal, still in water, lies overgrown but after a short distance comes to an end, having made way for new development. Johnson's Hillock Locks which were completed in 1816 were originally constructed to connect the new Leeds and Liverpool canal to the Lancaster at Whittle Springs Basin. The discovery by John Heyes of spring water in this area in 1836 led to the formation of the Whittle Springs brewery which flourished until 1929 when it merged with Nuttall's brewery of Blackburn. It became known as *'Lion Brewery'*.

Harry Blundell, a boatman from Whittle Springs talks about his working life on the canal 1915 – 1960 in the book *'Exploring our Waterway Heritage – A Boatman Remembers'*, published in the mid nineteen eighties. He says *"Away from Somerset House was the old canal; it is overgrown with reeds now but we delivered coal up there on our smaller boat. It was not as deep along there and they had two dredgers to keep it clear. Number 52 could turn round anywhere so that was always used……. The first wharf was at Navigation Bridge previously known as Johnson's Hillock Bridge. There used to be the Navigation Inn nearby but it is a house now and the canal ends at this point because of the new roads*

109

and the Central Lancashire New Town. Coal was delivered for Low Mill print works at the Navigation Bridge wharf and it was taken by horse and cart from there…….. The canal went over the River Lostock on an aqueduct after that, before it got to the two tunnels at Whittle. If your horse was too big the boat had to be pulled through them by the boatmen while his mate unhooked the horse and took it over the tunnels to the Duke of York Inn and back along the towpath to meet the boat when it emerged. There was a coal yard which we supplied at the Duke of York basin…..From there you came to Dock Bridge and the Summit basin. Older boatmen than me used to tell us about the coal deliveries to the Summit. In the old days it used to be sent along the tramway to Preston and later on it was sent by railway to Bamber Bridge. It is a pity that the canal with its tunnels and aqueduct has been allowed to decay and disintegrate. Soon there will be few traces that it was ever there".

Nearly twenty years later he has been proved right. One's progress in trying to find evidence of the *'old canal'* is hampered at every turn by new building and parts fenced off by private landowners although the determined walker will be able to trace parts of it from the *'Duke of York'*. Bi-centenary celebrations of the canal were held on the 1 June 2003 when many people came to witness the Mayor, Councillor Eric Bell unveil a commemorative plaque on Moss Bridge. There was a brass band, morris dancers and a guided walk to the Whittle tunnels.

Old canal at Whittle-le-Woods

THE SECOND CANAL AGE

What of the future of this canal that has had mixed fortunes in its efforts at restoration and keeping stretches of it open? *'The Lancaster Canal Trust'*, which was formed in 1963, have vigorously fought to keep the canal in water and to re-open closed sections.

Water to Tarmac

In Guild Year 1972 they successfully campaigned to stop the *'Central Lancashire Development Corporation's* proposals to use the line of the canal from Haslam Park to the terminus at Aqueduct Street for a new road. To celebrate their victory a rally was organised by the Trust, together with the Lancaster Boat Club and the Inland Waterway Association. Also that year saw the completion of the restoration of Ashton Basin, which had been badly neglected because of the threat of the road.

In 1990 the Trust formed a partnership with local authorities, British Waterways and other interested groups to form the *'Northern Reaches Restoration Group'* and in 2003 after extensive dredging by volunteers, a one mile stretch of canal was opened, seven miles north of the Northern terminus which enabled them to run their 28 ft narrowboat *'Waterwitch'* on Sundays and Bank Holidays during the summer.

To re-open the top fourteen miles of the canal is a huge project as it includes taking under the motorway in three places and re-watering the five miles of the *'dry'* bed to Kendal.

An article published on 28th June 2005 in the *'Lancashire Evening Post'* gave details of a plan to extend the canal from its current terminus in Shelley Road, Ashton, over Aqueduct Street on a new aqueduct across Fylde Road and ending at a marina at the now dereclict Maudland Bank, next to the university. This is all part of a wider, 20 year vision called the *'Riversway Project'* which will include a barrage and new river crossing.

The Lancaster leads

The most exciting canal project of recent times was the opening of the *'Millennium Ribble Link'* in September 2002. It connects the *'Lancaster'* with the Ribble Estuary so that boats can now cruise through the Link down the Ribble and Douglas rivers to the Rufford branch of the Leeds - Liverpool canal and then onto the rest of Britain's inland waterways. A celebration cruise to mark the event was held at Preston Riversway Marina with a flotilla of highly decorated boats.

One hundred and eighty three years earlier (1819) the first canal boat had reached the canal head at Kendal for its grand ceremonial opening where barges filled with grandly-attired passengers, bells ringing, flags hoisted on to public buildings, cannon fired at regular intervals, bands played and the procession of three packet boats and five barges set off to meet a contingent of barges from Lancaster. The full procession of sixteen boats arrived back at Kendal to be cheered by crowds of people.

Canal users, whether boaters, ramblers or anyone who enjoys the waterways have a lot to thank bodies such as the Lancaster Canal Trust and Inland Waterways Authority.

If you are interested in the future of our waterways and wish to join either of these organisations please contact the following:

Lancaster Canal Trust
Adrian Hughes
'Ilex'
Keasdale Road
Carr Bank
Milnthorpe LA7 7LH

Inland Waterways Association
FREEPOST NW2944
PO Box 114
Rickmansworth
WD3 1WD

www.lancastercanaltrust.org.uk

www.waterways.org.uk